I0528026

TaylorED Time

How to Dramatically Build Your Character & Live the Life FANTASTIC!*

*Full And Novel,
Thriving And Successful,
Totally In Control!

ANDREW S. TAYLOR

Copyright © 2022 by Andrew S. Taylor

TaylorED Time

How to Dramatically Build Your Character & Live the Life FANTASTIC!

All rights reserved.

No part of this work may be used or reproduced, transmitted, stored or used in any form or by any means graphic, electronic, or mechanical, including but not limited to photocopying, recording, scanning, digitizing, taping, Web distribution, information networks or information storage and retrieval systems, or in any manner whatsoever without prior written permission from the publisher.

Disclaimer: This book's intended purpose is not to substitute the medical advice of a physician or qualified therapist. The reader should regularly consult a physician in matters of their health and particularly in respect to any symptoms that may require diagnosis or medical attention.

CALVIN AND HOBBES © 1989 Watterson. Reprinted with permission of ANDREWS MCMEEL SYNDICATION. All rights reserved.

PEAK PRESS

An Imprint for GracePoint Publishing (www.GracePointPublishing.com)

GracePoint Matrix, LLC

624 S. Cascade Ave, Suite 201, Colorado Springs, CO 80903

www.GracePointMatrix.com

Email: Admin@GracePointMatrix.com

SAN # 991-6032

A Library of Congress Control Number has been requested and is pending.

ISBN: (Paperback) 978-1-955272-42-1

eISBN: 978-1-955272-43-8

Books may be purchased for educational, business, or sales promotional use.
For bulk order requests and price schedule contact:
Orders@GracePointPublishing.com

DEDICATION

Love & Gratitude!!

Mom & Dad

It is with my fully felt, whole heart, I say to all who love and support me,

THANK YOU!!

A+

"We do not believe in ourselves until someone reveals that deep inside us something is valuable, worth listening to, worthy of our trust, sacred to our touch. Once we believe in ourselves, we can risk curiosity, wonder, spontaneous delight or any experience that reveals the human spirit."

E. E. Cummings

TABLE OF CONTENTS

THOUGHTS FOR TODAY

Self-Help Books: Any one (book) will do and anyone (you) can do. My questions are "Will you impose your will?" and "Will you do your life's work?" I hope this one (book) and someone (you) will work for you. My unique approach with this book is how it parallels the same concepts and techniques used to build fictional characters in theater, TV, and movies with the building of non-fictional, real-life, everyday characters and people, a.k.a. *YOU!*

Question: If theater, TV, and movie artists, actors, and actresses can *magically* create whole new *fictional* characters and worlds, then why can't you also apply a little bit of your own MAGIC (Make A Good Intelligent Choice), and create a whole new, *non-fictional YOU?*

Answer: I believe you can. And I believe you will… *only if*…. You will achieve this result *only if* you totally commit to a practical process of personal growth, just like the one presented in this book. If you complete this journey successfully, then you will have positively produced your greatest masterpiece. You will have consciously created your *new and improved, real-life character.* And you will have MAGIC-ally manifested, your fully FANTASTIC (Full And Novel, Thriving And Successful, Totally In Control), self-helped self.

One Word's Definition: *holistic* [adj.] involving all of something; someone's all-encompassing everything. This includes all of someone's physical, intellectual, emotional, spiritual, solo, and social situations. This word commonly refers to using unusual, healthy, healing methodologies, i.e. practicing *holistic* medicine. But in this book, I abundantly apply this word to alternative applications and unconventional contexts.

TAYLORED TIME ACRONYMS

In this book you will find an abundance of acronyms. Use this list any time you need to know what one means.

BEAUTIFUL: Be yourself, Enlightened, Alive, Unique, Trustworthy, Intelligent, Faithful, and Unconditionally Loving!

EAT: Eat A Treat!

FANTASTIC: Full And Novel, Thriving And Successful, Totally In Control!

FEAR: False Expectations Apparent Realities

FUEL: Full-filling Unconditionally Enthusiastically Love

GIGSS: Gather In Group Support Systems

LRM: Lifetime Role Models

LOVE: Lots Of Vulnerable Emotions! Lots Of Vibrant Energies!

MAGIC: Make A Good Intelligent Choice

PIES: Physical Intellectual Emotional Spiritual

SOUL: Spirit Of Ultimate LOVE!

SORT: Self Occupations Relationships Time-Transitions

INTRODUCTION

CALVIN AND HOBBES © 1989 Watterson. Reprinted with permission of ANDREWS MCMEEL SYNDICATION. All rights reserved.

"It builds character." Clearly, this is not the first time Calvin has been presented this particular personal challenge. Nor will it be the last. And we can all relate to Calvin's complaint. Because at some point, we have all heard this poignant phrase and we have all questioned this commonly confronted concept. We ask ourselves:

- Who is this character I am building and creating?
- What mysterious force builds and creates this character?
- Where does this character building and creating take place?
- When should I be doing this character building and creating?
- Why am I doing all this character building and creating?
- How will the processes of this character building and creating work best for me and guarantee me living a success-full life?

This book is all about showing my methods for answering these very important life questions.

My method is simple. I take theatrical and *dramatic* character-building methodologies and I apply them to *real* life. This works! Today I live an efficiently organized, flexible-for-fun, time-managed, successful life. Every day above ground is a good day. Every day I do my best to make at least one, positive, conscious choice. This proactive, productive action, always gets me one step closer to achieving one of my many, primary life goals.

Now as easily as you opened this book, open your mind. Page-by-page, step-by-step, exercise-by-exercise, apply your will and do the work. I'm sure my methods will work for you. I'll talk the talk. You walk the walk!

THE 16 SECRETS OF SUCCESS

1. Holistically know yourself.

2. Find true (for you) north. Define your dreams and goals.

3. Use creative visualization. Make conscious choices. Map your projected life plan. Write everything down.

4. Take action immediately. Remember the NIKE slogan and Just Do It™.

5. Focus and pay attention.

6. Ask for help. Gratefully accept help. And earn all the help you are given.

7. How you think is everything. Eliminate negatives. Think only positives.

8. Be a lifelong learner.

9. Learn to see and analyze all life's little details. Learn from your mistakes. Follow the flow until all life lessons are learned.

10. Organize your life. Find a system that works for you.

11. Create a clear picture of the world. See how it is all connected.

12. Adjust your attitude. Empower your passion. Eliminate forecasting FEARs (False Expectations Apparent Realities)! Do what FUELs (Full-filling Unconditionally Enthusiastically Love) you!

13. Be perceptive from your perspective! Be persistent to your purpose! Never settle for *only* content and comfortable. *Also,* always strive for holistically happy and hungry! *Never give up! ... Don't quit! ... EVER!*

14. Get GIGSS (Gather In Group Support Systems). Take total responsibility for your life. Make a commitment to playing the lead-er part of *Your Life!* Live your life so self-improvement and acts of altruism are synonymous!

15. Celebrate family and friends! Create unity and community! Tap into your SOUL (Spirit Of Ultimate LOVE (Living Only Vibrant Energies))! Live the Life FANTASTIC (Full And Novel, Thriving And Successful, Totally In Control)!

16. Presentize yourself! Go back to number one. Start over!

A GUIDE FOR HOW TO USE THIS BOOK

CHAPTER 1: CHARACTER CRYSTALLIZATION! First, you will get crystal clear about your present-day character. You will remember where you are from and you will establish where you are right now. Then you will determine where you want to go.

CHAPTER 2: HUMAN BEING VS. HUMAN DOING! Second, you will travel through four stages of self-improvement. You will learn the difference between *being*—with *potential* energy—and *doing*—with *kinetic* energy. And in the last two sections you will learn why it is so important to focus and pay attention, and why, when you receive help, you must always earn it!

CHAPTER 3: SEE THE SCENE! Third, you will see the big picture, find your place in it, discover the real meaning of the word BEAUTIFUL (Be (yourself,) Enlightened, Unique Alive, Trustworthy, Intelligent, Faithful, and Unconditionally Loving), and, as the old Salt-N-Pepa song says, "Let's Talk About Sex!" Then, through thoughtful insight, and some safe-sex soul-searching, you will determine your character's potential for holistic intimacy (in-to-me-you-see). And, in the last section, you will learn four fundamental life lessons and you will see how school is always in session!

CHAPTER 4: SET THE STAGE! Fourth, you will SORT your life into a four-file system: Self, Occupations, Relationships, and Time-Transitions. You will learn the value of solo time and you will realize the difference between being emotionally lonely versus only being physically alone. You will follow the process of selecting lifetime role models and you will see how you must always MAGIC (Make A Good Intelligent Choice). You will sail the seven Cs when you Collect Cool Companions and Consciously Choose them with Clear Criteria! You will develop a whole-world, whole-humanity, global point of view. And in the last section, you will set your mind's set. You will create your own reality and you will know an absolute total truth: Fact *and* fiction, it takes all kinds to make a world!

CHAPTER 5: THE HEART OF YOUR ART! Fifth, you will fortify your attitude and passions! You will eliminate forecasting FEAR (False Expectations Apparent Realities)! You will determine what FUELs (Full-filling Unconditionally Enthusiastically Love) you! You will develop your stage presence. You will be perceptive from your perspective and persistent to your purpose! And finally, you will no longer, for-ever-more, simply settle for only being content and comfortable. Instead, you will consciously choose to steadfastly strive toward the glorious goal of living your life holistically happy and hungry!

CHAPTER 6: THE CURTAIN CALL! Sixth, your *New and Improved*, real life character will be positively produced. Shakespeare said, "All the world's a stage." So take a bow and make a dramatic promise to yourself by saying out loud, "In the play of my life, I WILL ALWAYS BE THE LEAD-ER!" And as the lead-er, in the sections Character Conclusions and Character Continuations, you will create *your* definition of success and *your My Mission Statement* to match. With these two items solidly set in writing, you will take complete responsibility for your life, you will get GIGSS (Gather In Group Support Systems), you will collectively celebrate family and friends, and you will consciously create unity and community. And now that the curtain call is done, like any actor or actress, you can start the process all over again.

CHAPTER 7: BEHIND THE SCENES AND EPILOGUE! Here at the close is where *our* joyful journey emphatically ends! *We* will collectively celebrate with a final fanfare and you will tap into your SOUL (Spirit Of Ultimate LOVE (Living Only Vibrant Energies))! Then you will royally reward yourself for totally taking this tremendous trip by throwing an all-out, enlightened ensemble, life-time-love-a-lots, constellation-of-characters, cast party! You will boldly begin *your* joyful journey to holistically *Live the Life FANTASTIC (Full And Novel, Thriving And Successful, Totally In Control)!*

And since you have *TaylorED Time: How to Dramatically Build Your Character & Live the Life FANTASTIC!* in your hands, you should know there is also a companion workbook. And you should also know that using the *TaylorED Time Workbook: How to Be the Captain of Your Character's Creation*, will greatly give you the opportunity to totally enhance, enrich, and empower your experience of everything!

All right! Action! Everything is set! Sit down. Get completely comfortable. Get gloriously geeked. And turn the page! *Our* journey is about to begin!

CHAPTER 1:
CHARACTER CRYSTALLIZATION!

Preview

All right! Action! Scene 1! In this chapter you will get crystal clear about who you are right now. Today it is time to do Character Crystallization. In this process you will do what many actors and actresses do first when they are cast in a role: they complete a Character and Self-Inventory. In Part One you will do extensive question and answer sessions about your life's story and pre-script. (A pre-script is a character's complete back-story, before their first appearance on stage or screen). Then you will write a short nature versus nurture mini-autobiography. In Part Two you will do a hands-on exercise which will show you how to create your Fact Foundation PIES (Physical Intellectual Emotional Spiritual) Chart. In Part Three you will prepare to audition for the real role of *Your Life* and you will complete your Holistic Life Resumé.

With your life's story and pre-script written out and organized, you will, as my old drama coach used to say, "Make your first entrance from the page to the stage." In real reality world terms, you will gratefully open the gift of your present, and you will presentize yourself.

Next, you will ask yourself the hardest question of all. In the drama world it is "What is my character's motivation?" In the real world it is "What do I want?" *This is what matters most to you!* And in the Find True (For You) North section, you will determine *today's* answer to this ultimate question.

1

In the chapter's final section, you will cast off your dock lines, determine your destination, and successfully set sail! In drama world terms, the actor or actress memorizes and/or improvises his or her script lines, (Sorry writers. There are *always* rewrites.), starts their character arc, and begins their rehearsal process. In real-world terms, you will learn how to center yourself, organize your information, and use creative visualization to map your Projected Life Plan. Then you will immediately take your first action step toward implementing your plan and amazingly achieving all your primary life goals.

Remember, the bottom-line truth is: If you want to change the world, *you* are the easiest place to start.

Character and Self-Inventory

Actors and actresses audition, do screen tests, and/or are sent scripts to read for possible character consideration. As soon as they accept a role, they break the script down, take it all apart, and through a series of specific questions, they complete a Character Inventory. The nature of the questions is usually dictated by which school of thought has predominantly influenced the actor or actress. Outside To Inside is what information is gathered by looking at the character's external appearance, actions, or dialogue; a.k.a. the book's cover. Inside To Outside is what information is discovered about the character's internal, intellectual thoughts, emotional manifestations, and their spiritual self; a.k.a. the book's content. The simplest single question one needs to ask is "Does the costume make the character or does the character make the costume?"

Five Example Questions from the Outside-To-Inside School:

1. What is the physical build and stature of the character?

    Examples: slender, athletic, toned, muscular, average, overweight, etc.

2. How does the character walk and physically carry themself?

    Examples: fast, slow, upright, stooped, stable, limping, etc.

3. What is the character's costume, including accessories and props? Are they functional, fashionable, and/or age appropriate?

    Examples: gun, pens, briefcase, back/fanny-pack, stethoscope, purse, hand bag, makeup, jewelry, wallet, glasses, keys, tie, scarf, gloves, shoes, boots, suspenders, utility/basic-belt, uniform/hard-hat, gear/ equipment-sports, etc.

4.   Is the character clearly from a specific race or ethnic background? If yes, how can you tell?

Examples: skin color, speech patterns, accents, social mannerisms, cultural costume choices, etc.

5.   Is the character clearly from a specific class or social status? If yes, how can you tell?

Examples: clothes, hair, hygiene, clean, dirty, new, used, designer or department store, generic or brand names, etc.

Five Example Questions from the Inside-To-Outside School:

1.   How intelligent is the character? Is he or she book and/or street smart? Have they achieved a high level of formal education and/or are they extremely experienced in The School of Life?

2.   What's the character's temperament? Are they calm, cool, and collected, or do they lack major emotional management skills?

3.   What is the character's emotional range/depth? Wide or narrow? Shallow or deep?

4.   Does the character have morals, a code of honor, ethics, and/or scruples?

5.   Does the character have a positive or negative self-image, which is matched with a high or low level of self confidence and self-esteem? What are the reasons, and/or origin stories, which answer these questions?

The number and complexity of these questions depends on the character being built. If it is a superficial stereotype then it only takes a few basic questions. But if it is a complex principal or a lead character, then the actor or actress really needs to do his or her homework. In the drama world there are two sources for answering these characterization questions: black and white script facts and conscious choice script interpretations. Taken from the teachings of Konstantin Stanislavski, (the father of method acting,) an English stage play director once said to me, "Acting is filling in all of the white space on a page." This is the best explanation of acting I have ever heard.

Now I know what you are thinking; you are silently saying, "How does all this apply to me in the real world?" Well clearly you do not have the luxury of having a fact-full, complete script of *Inside the Actors Studio* or *This Is Your Life*. But what you do have is a free-fair all-access pass to your own mind's memories. And the next three sections are all specifically designed to help ask *yourself* all the right questions. After a short walk down memory lane, you will have gathered and discovered all the necessary and pertinent information for you to know all your character's components. And when that is definitively done, you will easily and effortlessly, put together your own Self-Inventory.

Part One: Nature vs. Nurture

This section is based on some age-old questions: "How much of life is predetermined by genetic heritage, a.k.a. *nature?*" and "How much of life is dependent on one's environment, a.k.a. *nurture?*" Now do not worry, answering these major monumental, philosophical life questions, is not your homework. But you can understand a great deal about yourself when you look back into each one of these resource-full character libraries when you do the first exercise.

An example of a genetic character comparison is my own *relative* relationship with sugar. In the not-so-distant past, whenever I drank tea or coffee, the quantity of sugar which went into the drink, would have put any diabetic directly into insulin shock. However, when this astronomical amount is compared to *my mother's* childhood sweet-tooth stories, I come out looking simply sour. Now, not only do I know my own present-day character traits and tendencies, but I also know their past origins. And the more you know about yourself, the better equipped you will be to change and improve yourself in the future. To continue and complete my sweet sugar example, seeing my own habits and knowing my mother had the exact same habits, I now know to *limit* my sugar intake so as to support my present and future, holistic health.

This same rule also applies to examples from how you were nurtured. Your present-day character was shaped and built by your past story of life experiences. As a tangible means for further self-study, create a mini autobiography by completing the following exercise:

Exercise 1 - Nature vs. Nurture: Pre-Script and Life History

Step 1: List ten *Character Traits* (CT)* and their *Relative Origin* (RO)*.

Example: CT - I have a super sweet tooth. RO - I inherited this from my mother.

	CT	RO
1	_____	_____
2	_____	_____
3	_____	_____
4	_____	_____
5	_____	_____
6	_____	_____
7	_____	_____
8	_____	_____
9	_____	_____
10	_____	_____

*Overachievers should continue this list on a separate piece of paper.

Step 2: List ten *Character Traits* (CT)* and their *Historical Origin* (HO)*.

Example: CT - I am a very loyal friend. HO - I have at least four friends whom I have known for more than twenty years. And two I have known for over forty!

	CT	HO
1	_____	_____
2	_____	_____
3	_____	_____
4	_____	_____
5	_____	_____
6	_____	_____
7	_____	_____
8	_____	_____
9	_____	_____
10	_____	_____

* Overachievers should continue this list on a separate piece of paper.

Step 3: Use all your researched information to write a mini-autobiography. Use this title.

Lifelines of My Lifetime

_____

_____

_____

_____

_____

_____

_____

_____

_____

_____

_____

_____

_____

_____

_____

_____

_____

_____

_____

_____

*Overachievers should continue this life story on a separate piece of paper.

If you have never done an exercise like this one, keep going. After you have exhausted all your ideas, put it down for a day. Pick it up tomorrow and do it again. This way, over a relatively short period of time, maybe a week or two, you will have put together part one of your three-part, comprehensive, Self-Inventory. Save the results of this exercise as a hard copy or a computer document. Save the results in a folder entitled My Fact Foundation File.

If you are an overachiever who has kept a life-long journal, and/or a daily diary, and you know every branch and leaf of your family tree, then by all means keep up the good work. Of course, you can *also* continue to use these personal resources of important information. *But be careful!* Make sure you do not get lost in the vast variety of notebooks and "past pages." Make sure you do not spend your entire, extremely valuable, present-day lifetime, living in your old family tree house.

This section is specially designed to encourage you to trace the origins of a few more of your unique character traits. Take as much time as you need to feel comfortable with the amount of information you have gathered. Do not move on to Part Two until you feel completely confident you know yourself in Part One. Remember, this is *your* character *you* are building. *This is your life! You* pick the pace for *your* personal growth. *You* run *your* race, on *your* road, on *your* joyful journey, to *your* fantastic finish line of successful self-improvement!

Part Two: Fact Foundation PIES Chart

For me it is an easy choice. Out of the vast variety of flavors and types, by far, my favorite kind of pie is banana-cream. It is sweet, scrumptiously creamy, and because of the bananas, you can easily fool yourself into believing the pie does in fact have some nutritional value.

For this section, choose a favorite food which meets the following criteria:

- It is circular and it can be divided into four equal portions.
- It does not break the rules of any special dietary needs or plans.
- It is for you a culinary treat, luxury, and no-regrets reward.
- It can be eaten while reading and writing.
- Its culinary value will not diminish during the time it takes for you to complete this section, i.e. it will not get cold, melt, or spoil.

My favorite food of choice is _____.

Write it down. Get up. Go get it!

Good. Yes. Yummy! You have your favorite food of choice ready to eat. Now, divide it into four equal portions, and prepare yourself for a TaylorED Time original concept. *Today, you will complete the following exercise and you will eat—both at the same time!*

Exercise 2 - PIES (Physical Intellectual Emotional Spiritual): A Four-Letter Character Study

Step 1: Take one portion of your favorite food and set it down just out of arms' reach. Or even better, put it on the other side of the room.

Step 2: Answer all the questions from Letter 1 below. Rewrite the questions and answer them on a separate piece of paper. Save the results of this exercise in your Fact Foundation File.

Step 3: EAT (Eat A Treat)!

Step 4: Repeat steps 1, 2, and 3 for Letters 2, 3, and 4.

Letter 1 - Physical: These questions refer to your physical body, as it first appears to a theater audience or to a real life, casual observer. For clarification, go back to the Character and Self-Inventory section and review the Five Example Questions from the Outside-To-Inside School.

Physical Questions:

1. What is your walk?
2. What is your talk?
3. What is your size and shape?
4. Are you in or out of shape?
5. What is your publicly presented gender?
6. What are your visible props and accessories?
7. Do you have glasses, contacts, or unnatural colored contacts?
8. What do your face, skin, teeth, and smile look like?
9. What is your hairstyle and color?
10. What are your clothing, jewelry, and make-up color schemes?
11. What are your everyday and special occasion personal looks?

12. Are you clearly from a specific ethnicity or cultural heritage? If yes, how could someone tell?

13. Are you clearly from a certain socioeconomic class or social status? If yes, how could someone tell?

14. Do you look your age? Why or why not?

15. Do you have healthy hygiene?

16. Do you talk with your body and gesticulate with your hands?

17. What does your body language tell people?

18. Do you carry yourself with bad or good posture?

19. Do you have any disabilities? If yes, what are your disability compensation needs?

20. Do you have a noticeable physical presence, or, as a wallflower, do you blend into the crowd, to the point of being virtually invisible?

Add your own Physical Questions. Keep going. Do not stop until you feel satisfied you have totally completed this part of the exercise.

Letter 2 - Intellectual: These questions refer to your basic mental capabilities. For clarification on Parts 2, 3, and 4, go back to the Character and Self-Inventory section and review the Five Example Questions from the Inside-To-Outside School.

Intellectual Questions:

1. Are you an educated person?

2. Are you book and/or street smart?

3. Do you have a good imagination and creative problem-solving skills?

4. What is your IQ? Do you hide it or show it to people?

5. Are you slow or quick-witted? How do you describe your sense of humor?

6. Do you have any disabilities? If yes, what are your disability compensation needs?

7. Do you have any special types of mental abilities or talents?

8. Do you know facts and figures in a specific area of expertise such as math and science, history and politics, arts and entertainment, or sports and recreation?

9. What type of memory do you use? Visual, auditory, or literary?

10. Do you have an efficient sensory memory for past sights, sounds, smells, tastes, and touches?

Add your own Intellectual Questions. Keep going. Do not stop until you feel satisfied you have totally completed this part of the exercise.

Letter 3 - Emotional: These questions refer to your emotional make-up. Even though most people associate emotions as external manifestations, for the purpose of this exercise emotions will be considered to be internal character traits.

Emotional Questions:

1. What is your temperament and general personality type?

2. Are you reserved or demonstrative with your emotions?

3. Are you on a level track, or are you on an emotional roller coaster that goes through dramatic highs and lows and quick-change loop-d-loops?

4. Are you emotionally limited and superficial, or do you have an extensive emotional range with great depth?

5. Are you a mystery or are you easy to read when you wear your heart on your sleeve?

6. Do your emotions control you or do you control your emotions?

7. Are you thick-skinned or super-sensitive?

8. Do you collect and carry emotional baggage or do you travel light?

9. Do you know your internal buttons and when they are being pushed?

10. Can you master and use your emotions to benefit yourself and others? Do you have emotional intelligence?

Add your own Emotional Questions. Keep going. Do not stop until you feel satisfied you have totally completed this part of the exercise.

Letter 4 - Spiritual: These questions refer to your holistic, spiritual self. This goes way beyond just your religious beliefs. It should also include your individual human spirit and your biggest-picture-possible, human race, spiritual point of view.

Spiritual Questions:

1.   What is your religious and/or cultural heritage upbringing? How and why are they different or the same?

2.   What are your present day religious and/or cultural beliefs? How and why are they different or the same?

3.   Is your self-confidence, self-esteem, self-image, self-nature, and spiritual self negative or positive?

4.   Are you confident your spiritual self will persevere, overcome, survive, and thrive?

5.   Do you have team spirit? Or are you self-sufficient?

6.   Do you feel you are apart from nature or are you a part of nature?

7.   Based on your belief system, do you have a secure set of morals, honor codes, ethics, and/or scruples?

8.   Are you a "doormat," or do you have the spirit, spine, and spunk to stand up for yourself?

9.   Are you a pessimist, realist, or optimist?

10.   Do you have faith in yourself? Do you have faith in the whole human race?

Add your own Spiritual Questions. Keep going. Do not stop until you feel satisfied you have totally completed this part of the exercise.

For all these questions, including any you may have added, every answer matters. Remember, the more facts you know about yourself and the more you are able to put into your Fact Foundation File, the stronger your character will be and the better equipped you will be to change and improve yourself in the near future. For this exercise, I encourage you to be extremely self-conscious. In fact, in this first chapter, that is the whole idea.

And now one more step ....

Step 5: Find a square bulletin board. Make sure it is big enough to display all your answers. Draw a circle that touches all four sides. Divide that into four equal pie sections. It should look like my banana cream pie or your four favorite slices of special sweetness. Post all your answers from all four parts. This is your Fact Foundation PIES (Physical Intellectual Emotional Spiritual) Chart. Save the chart until you are finished with Part Three: Your Holistic Life Resumé.

If you have the technological expertise to create a Fact Foundation PIES (Physical Intellectual Emotional Spiritual) Chart on your computer, with some kind of drawing or graphic design program, then by all means do it. Not only will you have my permission and encouragement, but you will also have my total, technological admiration.

Part Three: Your Holistic Life Resumé

A regular resumé contains a summary of information on an individual's education, work experience, special interests, and hobbies, etc. If you are a young adult and you have never written a resumé, then right now, take the time to put one together. You will need it to complete this section and you will certainly need it for any future job and/or career ambitions. (You can find several helpful templates and resources online.) If you are an experienced adult and you already have a resumé, then print it and post it right in the middle of your Fact Foundation PIES (Physical Intellectual Emotional Spiritual) Chart. You will definitely need your regular resumé to use as an outline skeleton for your Holistic Life Resumé.

Now instead of imagining you are on a typical job interview, even though you will be using your regular resumé to complete the job application, imagine you are on a first date or you are in that unique, get-to-know-each-other stage of a new relationship. Imagine you are courting yourself. Imagine you are auditioning for the real role of *Your Life*. Ask yourself all the personal questions, which only get asked in these singular situations. Do not be afraid to call yourself out and document all your intrinsic idiosyncrasies. Think of it this way: If your favorite actor or actress wanted to play the part of *A Perfect You*, then all these extra, tiny tidbits of bonus material would certainly fall into the category of being absolutely need to know. When you include all these special supplementary information items and data details in your regular resumé, the result will be your Holistic Life Resumé. Make sure it is complete. Just like Jamie Foxx has said in interviews about selecting roles he is interested in playing, make sure there is enough, "meat on the bones." Make sure you will get the job(s), you will keep the relationship(s), and you will get the real part of *Your Life*—a.k.a. *A Perfect You!*

The concept of *A Perfect You* originated when I said to a friend, "Nobody's perfect."

She said, "Oh on the contrary. *YOU are A Perfect You!* The only actor who could ever *perfectly* portray all your little imperfections *is you*." I knew she was right. And to this day, whenever I look in the mirror, I know the man looking back is *A Perfect Me!*

Now it is time for a total truth summary sentence. You have finished your three-part, Self-Inventory. Yes. You did the research and you traced your nature versus nurture character traits. You answered all your questions and you completed a hands-on exercise, which helped you create your Fact Foundation PIES (Physical Intellectual Emotional Spiritual) Chart. You added the Jamie Foxx, "meat on the bones," onto your regular resumé, and you successfully converted it into a Holistic Life Resumé. With this written three-part Self-Inventory all assembled and displayed as a visual aid, you are certainly set to move forward into the next section of this chapter. It is time to gratefully open the gift of your present. It is time to presentize yourself!

Presentize Yourself!

In the drama world, actors and actresses have countless catchphrases, which are synonymous with this concept. Examples include: "Be in the moment." "ACT NOW!" and "Center yourself in the scene." In the real world, the closest self-help taught thought is communicated when you are told the total truth and given the following absolutely accurate advice: "Live in the present. It is the only real time there is." Presentize is my catchphrase word for living in the greatest gift of all—*the present!*

Usually when an actor or actress creates a character, they have read, and/or improvised their script, memorized their lines, set their blocking, (how they will move around the stage or set,) and done extensive amounts of background research and/or homework. With this in mind, it is the director's responsibility to keep them honest and whenever necessary to tell them, "Do not act in your character's future. It cheats him or her out of their present moments. Always remember in the real life of your character, you really do not know what you are going to say or do next. It all has to appear as if it is evolving naturally in real time."

So, in *your* real life, be your own director. Remind yourself you can only live your life moment-to-moment, and *you real-ly do not definitively know* your unforeseeable future. Do this whenever you get stuck repetitively thinking and replaying past events or future fantasies over and over again in your head. Stop yourself from getting obsessively loopy. Stop yourself when you are totally lost, whimsically wandering in the mazes of your mind. The reason for this reminder is when you do find yourself engaging in these momentary mind freeze-frames, you are actually unknowingly cheating yourself out of the greatest gift:

your real life present. John Lennon is often quoted as having so smartly said, "Life, (or the present,) is what happens while you're busy making other plans (for the future.)" And to paraphrase Disney's *The Lion King*, our behind, (the past,) is behind us, so leave it behind.

With the creation and completion of your three-part Self-Inventory you have answered two incredibly important life questions: Holistically, where did I come from? (What was my past?) and Who am I now? (What is my present?) Now that you know your present, open it up and live in it. Do not be afraid to see yourself as a total package. Reread your Fact Foundation File and take a good long look at yourself in a full-length mirror. *Know* today is truly the first and *only* day of the rest of your life. *Know* you are ready, willing, and able to live it.

And also know you can now move forward and do the last two sections of this chapter. You can easily find true (for you) north! And you can boldly set sail! As Jim Henson, the ingenious innovator of The Muppets, often said, "Take what you've got and fly with it!"

Find True (For You) North!

For centuries, the North Star was a sailor's guiding light. With its unchanging position in the sky, sailors could always count on it to show them the way home. On starless, cloud-covered nights, sailors could also use four specific tools: compasses, timekeepers, sextants, and maps. Being able to use these tools was literally vital, for without them, to be lost and out of sight of land, would certainly mean a loss of life.

In this same spirit, you need to find true (for you) north. What is your soul's way of life? How do you interact with people? How do you approach the world? What is your true nature? I answer these questions with: I am a *teacher*. And my life's code of conduct is based on a deep desire, to live and to love, as a *harmonizer*. These two words—*teacher* and *harmonizer*—describe my holistic life's character; this is true (for me) north.

I chose my two words through formal and informal means—using old, forever used tools like psychometric tests and doing new, original exercises like what I am sharing with you in this book. There are countless examples of these "personality tests" and formal systems to help you understand yourself. A personal favorite is The Color Code Personality Test. If you search online using this title, along with the keywords blue, gold, orange, and green, you will find the test's website. You can also find several self-help book references on my website's Recommended Reading List. And as you do the next exercise, use the following Seneca quote for inspiration: "No wind is favorable if you do not know the direction, or port, for which you are heading."

15

Exercise 3 - True (For You) North Task Time

Step 1: Do an internal gut check. Ask yourself if you already know your true north. If you do, write it down.

Step 2: If you do not, do external research and determine your own destination. You can find personality, and/or vocation tests online, at a local library, or at a nearby college or university's Career Planning & Placement Office. Three reference books for this purpose include:

What Color is Your Parachute? by Richard Nelson Bolles

How to Find the Work You Love by Laurence G. Boldt

Zen and The Art of Making a Living by Laurence G. Boldt

Whatever resources you use, clearly keep your goal in mind. You want to find true (for you) north. You want to answer the following questions: What is your motivation? and What do you want?

When you are able to answer these two questions, it means you have successfully determined your destination. So confidently take your first action step, cast off your restraining dock lines, and coast out of your presentized self's safe harbor. In short, self-assuredly set sail!

Set Sail!

Congratulations! You are your ship's captain. You control your holistic helm. You have determined your destination and you know true (for you) north. Your cargo is complete and you have everything you need to make your journey an absolute, sensational success... *almost.*

Before you can go beyond the harbor's last lookout point, and before you can safely lose sight of the shore, you need a map. In acting arts terms, you need to get a clear picture of your future. You need to conceive your character arc. In real world terms, you need to center yourself, organize your information, use creative visualization, and map your Projected Life Plan.

If presentizing yourself is a holistic act of completely knowing who you are today, then centering yourself is a specific act of totally being in the moment, right now. In addition to the acting arts world, centering yourself is universally used throughout all the martial arts. You can use the following quick and easy three-step process, whenever you need to be calm, cool, collected, and centered.

Exercise 4 - Centering Yourself: A Three-Step Process

Step 1: Concentrate on breathing slow and steady (12-14 breaths per minute).

Step 2: Center your body's energy just below and behind your belly button.

Step 3: Clear your mind, relax your body, and repeat as needed.

For more examples and explanations, see *The Way of Aikido: Life Lessons from an American Sensei* by George Leonard. This is one of many useful resources listed on my website's Recommended Reading List.

Here's some good news: your three-part Self-Inventory is all the material you will need to map your Projected Life Plan. And when it is ornately displayed, as a visual aid on a bulletin board or computer, it puts all your information in its most organized and user-friendly format. If you have been following instructions, your need-to-do task is already done. Of course, if you have not followed instructions… *yet*, then the bad news is, you still need to stay in your safe harbor and take all the time you need to properly complete your ship's outfitting.

For now, I will assume you are supremely ship shape. So the next step is for you to use creative visualization to create the map for your fantastic future. Professional athletes use this technique all the time as part of their pre-performance routine. In their mind's eye, they imagine themselves performing their team or individual sport, and they see themselves as a successful winner. In the same spirit, do the following exercise. Visualize your ideal version of a victorious, successful life and map your Projected Life Plan.

Exercise 5 - Creative Visualization: Manifest Your Mental Imagery

Step 1: Gather materials, i.e., paper, pens, pencils, palm pilot, tablet, or computer.

Step 2: Write your page headings. Use True (For You) North for all.

Step 3: Brainstorm. List all your future desires, wants, interests, and ideas.

Warning! Remember, these are *not* the future desires, wants, interests, and ideas which have been presented or spoon fed to you by your family, friends, school personnel, pushy peers, ambitious adults, and/or *everyone else but you!* Make sure these desires, wants, interests, and ideas *are created by you*. Make sure they are specifically designed to help you live *your* definition of a successful, happy life.

Step 4: Transfer and organize all your listed items into three categories, a.k.a. Greatness Goals: short-term goals, long-term goals, and lifetime achievements.

Step 5: Pause for station identification. Think of this as a theatrical, dramatic beat. This will give you time to think about and add any additional items.

Step 6: Finalize your lists. Sign and date them and make several copies.

Step 7: Distribute the copies to all your allies.

Note: It pays to advertise. And F.Y.I., *these lists are your written, Projected Life Plan!*

Step 8: Take action immediately. Pick an item from each list and every day take at least one action step, toward achieving at least one of your chosen life goals.

Okay. *Now* you have everything you need. You centered yourself. You organized your informational cargo. You did creative visualization. You put together a Self-Inventory map, which is your written Projected Life Plan. And now you *know*, all these things will lead you to a land where you will amazingly accomplish golden goals. You can now take the helm and set your heading to go far beyond the horizon. After a quick post view, you can set sail and stay the course. Your fantastic future is waiting for you in Chapter 2: Human Being vs. Human Doing! I am sure for you it will be filled with fun and many more magical moments of sensational self-discovery.

Post View

In the sultry style of Mae West, "Well, hello sailor!" Or with Billy Crystal's *Saturday Night Live* Fernando voice, "You look marvelous!" And I hope you also feel marvelous! Because by completing Chapter 1, you have come a long way on your joyful journey towards self-improvement.

For a moment, look back with self-admiration. You have completed the following seven sections:

- Character and Self-Inventory
- Part One: Nature vs. Nurture
- Part Two: Fact Foundation PIES (Physical Intellectual Emotional Spiritual) Chart
- Part Three: Your Holistic Life Resumé
- Presentize Yourself!
- Find True (For You) North!
- Set Sail!

You have completed the following five exercises:

- Nature vs. Nurture: Pre-Script and Life History
- PIES (Physical Intellectual Emotional Spiritual) A Four-Part Character Study
- True (For You) North: Task Time
- Centering Yourself: A Three-Step Process
- Creative Visualization: Manifest Your Mental Imagery

You have completed four of The 16 Secrets of Success:

1. Holistically know yourself.

   You have gone through the process of putting together a three-part Self-Inventory. You know your nature versus nurture. You have created a tangible, written, visual aid, Fact Foundation PIES (Physical Intellectual Emotional Spiritual) Chart, and you have created a Holistic Life Resumé. This resumé shows you the Jamie Foxx "meat on the bones" of your complete character.

2. Find true (for you) north. Define your dreams and goals.

   You have done what you needed to do to find true (for you) north! And you have set sail! You are going past the horizon of your dramatic dreams and Greatness Goals.

3. Use creative visualization. Make conscious choices. Map your projected life plan. Write everything down.

   You have completed each one of these sub-steps.

4. Take action immediately. Remember the NIKE slogan and Just Do It™.

   You have completed this step within Exercise 5, Step Eight: Take action immediately. And you have done all these things successfully! *YOU GO! YOU ARE THE CHARACTER! A.K.A. A PERFECT YOU!*

Okay. Now before we move on to Chapter 2, here's a short story of my magnum opus's origin ....

My Elite Example: I Know This Works!

As a special day event keynote speaker, I gave my TaylorED Time presentation to a small group of high school seniors. First, I guided the students through the seven sections of Chapter 1. This was the foundation for my two-hour presentation. Then, I did an audience participation exercise.

I invited twenty students to join me on stage to form a chorus line. I gave each one a 4x6 index card and a pencil. I told them to write their name, five external character traits, and five internal character traits. Then I put their collected cards in a, "magic sorting hat." (This was way before Harry Potter.)

Then, I presented them with a challenge. I told them how Peter Sellers, the original Inspector Clouseau, once said, "When I created a character's walk and talk, that's when I knew I had him set." Then I said, "My challenge to you is to choose somebody else's character card from the hat, think of one line to say, and dramatically walk their walk, and talk their talk."

At one end of the line, was a girl who described herself with these words on her character card: four feet six inches tall, owl glasses, petite, pretty, girly girl, book smart, invisible, introverted, and shy. A wallflower, who was very independent and self-sufficient. At the other end of the line, there was a boy with these words written on his card: six feet four inches tall, twenty-twenty vision, bright blue eyes, 3XL, hot and handsome, street smart, very visible, extroverted, confident, life of the party, team leader. He was socially recognized and rewarded as a natural winner. Guess who picked whose name out of the magic sorting hat?

That's right! As I watched the students read their chosen cards, I saw the small girl's face and body language go into an instant state of pre-panic attack. So I quickly walked over and asked to see her card. As soon as I read it, I immediately knew the reason for her rapidly approaching anxiety. I quickly and gently reminded her, "Don't panic. Don't worry. You are one hundred percent safe. Trust me. You will go last. And you are going to be great!"

Then, I gave all the other students about five minutes to brainstorm and rehearse their new character. While they were busy, I took the small girl backstage and softly said, "Remember what you have learned so far. You now have a clear picture of *your* character and who you are today. You will have about twenty minutes before it is your turn. So take the time and productively work it. Read *your new* character's card and simply make a choice. Take all the energy and confidence you can generate, and with passion, enthusiasm, and a real positive attitude, commit to your choice!" Remember, the Henry Ford and the Nike quotes. Henry Ford said, "Believe you can't or believe you can, either way you'll be right."

You are far better off if you believe you can succeed at performing this challenge. And Nike reminds us to, "Just Do It." So I encouraged her to believe in herself and just do it!

With an ever so small, sparkle in her eyes, and the slightest hint of a smile, she said in her soft, shaky, sweet voice, "Okay."

Twenty minutes later, after all the other students had presented their new characters and received their appropriate applause, that same small girl walked out on her tippy toes, with her chin up, her shoulders back, and with a visible energy, which made her seem larger than life—*she glowed!* When she got to center stage, she put both hands up in the air, took a deep breath, and shouted at the top of her lungs, "I AM A 3XL, HOT, HANDSOME, HUNK, MACHO MAN, STREET SMART, VERY VISIBLE, EXTROVERT, CONFIDENT, LIFE OF THE PARTY, GREAT GROUP/TEAM LEADER, AND SOCIALLY RECOGNIZED, REWARDED, NATURAL, ALL TIME WINNER!" … WOW! … And before she could even take one single step towards the stage left exit, the whole audience erupted into a wild, cheering, standing ovation! Even the captain of the varsity basketball team, the real-life character, who she had just clearly and confidently impersonated, was very visibly impressed!

After giving her a few minutes to bask in her miraculous moment, I joined her on stage. We took a few deep breaths together to calm the scene, and then I looked her in the eyes and said, "First. *Never forget this moment!* You will be able to use this magical memory for the rest of your life. Second. *Always remember there is absolutely nothing wrong with your present character and who you are right now!* The only difference between who you are right now and who you were twenty minutes ago, is *now your character is no longer a matter of chance; it is a matter of choice! IT IS YOUR CHOICE!*" There was a petite pause and suddenly she had an incredibly illuminated, abundantly enlightened, Aha! moment. With her now big, bright, blue eyes, and the biggest full-of-new-life smile I have ever had the extreme pleasure of seeing on a sweet face, *she winked at me*, and said, in her now, noticeably new, strong, confident, and crystal-clear voice, "Okay!"

I can solidly say, beyond a shadow of doubt, when that young lady left the stage, two lives were changed forever: hers and mine! I promise it was a VERY special day event, which I am sure I will remember for the rest of my life!

Okay. Now turn the page. Our journey continues in Chapter 2: Human Being vs. Human Doing!

CHAPTER 2:
HUMAN BEING VS. HUMAN DOING!

Preview

All right! Action! Scene 2! In Chapter 1, you completed Character Crystallization. In Chapter 2, you will keep the process moving forward and upward. You will continue your real life's character creation. And you will build on your now crystal-clear fact foundation. You will learn about four stages of self-improvement. And you will ultimately discover the difference between a Human Being vs. Human Doing!

The first stage of self-improvement is comatose versus conscious. This stage is where most people *exist*. I believe about seventy percent exist in a comatose state. And that is on a good day! Ten percent are in the second stage, asleep versus awake. Another ten percent live in the third stage of aware versus alive. The fourth stage, which contains the last ten percent of the planet's population, is mind-full versus mind-free. When artists and musicians, athletes and coaches, and actors and actresses, find themselves living in this stage, they are sometimes described as being in the zone. In simpler terms, they have successfully bridged the gap between human being and human doing.

The next section is Focus and Pay Attention! Here you will read about four focus factors. And you will learn special techniques to enhance your concentration. When you use this information in your daily life, you will significantly improve your ability to focus. And you will dramatically increase your aptitude for paying attention.

The last section is Help: Earn It! For some people the last thing on Earth they'd ever seriously want to do is ask for, and actually accept, help. In this section, you will learn early on in the process, how and why not to be one of these self-defeating individuals. You will learn how to ask for, and graciously receive, help. And you will also learn the importance of when you are given help, how you must always, absolutely earn it.

Comatose vs. Conscious

The first stage of self-improvement results from being energetically comatose. I am using this term to describe people who are just wandering through their lives and are unconsciously reacting to their routine circumstances. I am sure you will easily recognize these zoned-out zombies. You may already know a few, professionally and/or personally. I believe about seventy percent of the planet's population *exists* in this first stage and I specifically use this word, because as I see it, being in this stage *is not really living* in the strictest sense of the word.

When actors and actresses fall into and get stuck in this comatose stage, it can be highly harmful to daily production of their art and craft. It can go so far as to be deadly to their careers. Either way, getting conscious as you did in Chapter 1 is virtually vital.

Now, just for the sake of building up your own self-esteem, take yourself through the next exercise. Judge for yourself. Compare your new, conscious self to everyone around you. Recognize the difference between comatose nomads and relatively conscious characters.

Exercise 6 - Comatose vs. Conscious: Clear Comparisons

Step 1: Be conscious. Observe everyone. This means strangers, acquaintances, friends, and family.

Step 2: Be objective. Based on how individuals interact, put people in two categories: *Actors* and *Re-Actors*.

Step 3: After a self-determined period of time, when you think you have collected enough data, count your numbers and review your results. I predict you will find a 2:1 ratio of *Re-Actors* to *Actors*, a.k.a. *almost seventy percent!*

Congratulations! As an *Actor* or *Actress*, you are in the top thirty percent of the planetary population. Welcome to the land of the *living!* And since you are living, or in this case reading, in the world of a self-help book, I hope this conscious realization gives you the opportunity to take stock and count your blessings. Do not worry. No one will ever actually accuse you of being an elitist. After all, you are still being a realist. And in the real world, you are really and fully being conscious.

A Quintessential Quote: This is part of the intro of Shakti Gawain's book *Awakenings*. I am including it because it parallels the chapter points and it says what needs to be said as an example for us all. Truth: "Many of us in the world today are on a consciousness journey. We are seeking to bring our individual and collective lives into greater alignment with natural laws and universal principles, so that we can live in balance and harmony with ourselves, others, and The Earth. Today, with the ecological, social, and political challenges we face, in addition to our own personal issues, it is essential that we learn to live more consciously. By individually taking responsibility to live our lives with awareness, we can set examples that will empower others in our world to do the same.

Learning to live our daily lives with consciousness is an ongoing, ever deepening, lifetime process. It requires that we contact essential spiritual wisdom and integrate it into all other levels of our being and doing - physical, intellectual, emotional, and spiritual. It challenges us to recognize and release old patterns and beliefs and to open up to new ways in every area of our lives."

Asleep vs. Awake

I would hope everyone in the modern-day medical profession could readily recognize the difference between someone who is ultimately unconscious versus someone who is merely asleep. When it comes to a clearly conscious person, who is simply sleep-walking through life or just going through the motions, I imagine the difference between being *metaphorically* asleep, versus being *holistically awake* is much more subtle.

When an actor or actress plays a scene opposite someone who is seemingly asleep, versus someone who is absolutely awake, and fully in the moment, they experience an extremely dramatic difference in the partner's energy level. In the real world, as you grow and build your character, be conscious of the people with whom you are acting. Be courteous and raise your energy level to a point where it is overtly obvious, *you are awake!*

Aware vs. Alive

The difference between aware and alive is best explained by considering the main character in Brian Clark's play *Whose Life Is It Anyway?* (In the movie, Richard Dreyfuss played the part to perfection.) Ken Harrison is a sculptor. After a terrible car crash, Ken wakes up in the hospital completely paralyzed from the neck down. He suddenly realizes the only times in his life when he ever felt truly alive were sculpting and being with a woman, *and he will never feel or experience either, ever again.* In short, he is completely aware of his situation. After this realization sets in, he consciously chooses to attempt to force the hospital to discharge him from their care. In essence, he is arguing to be allowed to die. The hospital sees this as an attempt to commit suicide, and they question his sanity and his ability to make a rational, reasonable decision. He argues his case, and he rationally states how since he will never be truly alive again, reasonably he should be allowed to have control over the end of his life. Especially since, by *his* definition, he wants much more out of life, and now from his point of view, his life has become a physical, intellectual, emotional, and spiritual, permanently painful, non-life. He ultimately wins his freedom of choice, and so he discharges himself from the hospital. He chooses to die on his own terms. The movie's moral is, for some, *simply being aware of one's life is not enough. They also need to feel fully, absolutely, and abundantly alive!*

Mind-Full vs. Mind-Free

Mind-full versus mind-free is the hardest stage to achieve. It requires extreme levels of commitment, dedication, practice, and ultimately performance. It also clearly shows the difference between routinely reacting as a human being and alive-ly acting as a human doing. The following are three prime-time examples:

1. Artists and Musicians: When artists and musicians first start, they say they are, "practicing" their craft or instrument. Only when they are mind-full of an adequate amount of theory and techniques, are they able to mind-free-ly transcend all the activities and notes. In that state, they can automatically create authentic works of art and/or make melodic music, and they can forever after confidently claim they are abundantly able to purposely produce their art, or positively play their instrument.

2. Athletes and Coaches: Also with, "practice," athletes and coaches can become mind-full of an adequate amount of special skills, rules, regulations, techniques, and talents associated with a single sport. But only when they reach a mind-free level of performance can it be smartly said, they are actually able to play the sport.

Note: These two groups often describe this concept in terms of different memory types. Explicit memory is relating to things they know internally and intellectually. Examples include: being mind-full and knowing a lot of artistic modalities, musical theory, all the rules of a specific sport, and/or how to technically produce sound with a particular instrument. Implicit memory, sometimes called motor or muscle memory, can only be mind-free and is externally shown by effortlessly and intuitively doing the actions.

3.   Actors and Actresses: When "practicing" in the theater or movie world, the aim is to have dialogue, emotion, and positioning so ingrained that it shifts from being mind-full—needing a script or prompter—to mind-free where you can step fully into a character. In live theater it is being able to respond unscripted to something happening on stage. In movie making, through the process of rehearsing, discovering, and doing extra takes, the cast might find themselves improvising and discovering, "happy accidents."

As a child, adolescent, and adult actor, I have had the extreme pleasure to experience several, mind-free moments on stage. The following story describes my most memorable, mind-free moment: Patrick, my twenty-year best friend and un-biological brother, died in a terrible truck accident. He was not wearing a seat belt. He hit a curb, lost control, and rolled into a ditch. He was thrown out and pinned underneath. He died on August 1st, 1998. His body and my heart were completely crushed.

On October 1st, I moved from Illinois to Michigan. I needed to heart-fully heal, and I needed to geographically start a new chapter in my life. The ideal opportunity arrived in the form of a local community theater's production of Mary Chase's *Harvey*. When I was twelve, Patrick described me as, "a cross between Elwood P. Dowd [the play's main human character] and Kermit the Frog." So, on December 1st, I auditioned. I didn't just read the lines and react to the other people, I acted the part and played perfectly with the other performers.

Elwood's best friend Harvey is a Pooka. This is a magical, selectively invisible, and often mischievous creature from Celtic mythology. It usually takes animal form, in this case, a rabbit. It usually befriends, "rum-pots or crackpots." Elwood is both, and his Pooka is unusually large. Elwood sees it as about, "six-foot three, not including the ears." Well, I am not a, "rum-pot" but I have been called, "eccentric" a time or two, and as for the description of Harvey, I must say, it fit Patrick to a T—minus the ears of course! And to have Patrick on stage with me, at least in sweet spirit, was happily holistically healing.

My most memorable mind-free moment was during a particular *Harvey* performance. It was late March, the snow on the old theater roof was melting, so there were several large leaks in the dressing room, green room, ticket office, lobby, and actually on stage! The cast and crew did their best to fix and/or contain the leaks, but the unwanted, wet event was inevitable. During my major monologue scene, a fountain faucet of run-off water came pouring down on the stage. It was dripping on a desk and splatter splashing all over the floor. There was no way to effectively ignore it. Fortunately, I was so mind-full of my character, I was easily able to mind-free-ly ad-lib. So, I stretched my hand forward, touched the water, looked up, and I said, "Oh well, I guess in every life a little rain must fall." Since *the scene was set inside*, the audience was able to acknowledge the leak, laugh out loud, and we were able to graciously go on with the scene without too much "Don't look at the big, wet, pink elephant in the middle of the room." The water did not become a debilitating distraction. It was a dramatic, magical, mind-free moment, which I am sure I will remember for the rest of my life.

This unforgettable experience was way beyond beneficial because playing this dramatic character has had a profound and long-term effect on my real-life character. The following story shows how I took one of Elwood's key character traits and with a small, conscious choice, applied it directly to my every day, real life.

Throughout the rehearsal process I concentrated on creating Elwood's flip-phrase. This is a popular acting tool. It is a short phrase, which you say to yourself just before going on stage. Its main purpose is to help an actor or actress "flip" an internal switch and turn on the character's stage life energy.

On the morning of opening night, I woke up with the following realization: Elwood never sees his feet! Don't worry, I will explain. Elwood's friend Harvey is a, "mythical, magical creature that can see into the future." Harvey tells Elwood what is going to happen next, and it actually does happen. I figured since they are best friends, Harvey would certainly warn Elwood of any danger, or, at the very least, Harvey would protect Elwood and simply tell him how, for the rest of his life, everything is guaranteed to be great. In short, Elwood's life will be completely wonderful and absolutely one hundred percent safe and happy.

If someone, or something, like Harvey, ever informed me of this possibility, and subsequently, proved it to me, I believe that would be an ultimate act of total enlightenment. Just think, you would truly never have to worry about anything ever again. You would *know for a fact* you will never fall down a flight of stairs or trip on any unseen sidewalk curb. You could go anywhere, and meet anyone, without any fear whatsoever. You could confidently look up, and literally look forward to everything. You would *know*, you never need to look down to find your feet.

27

So, to this day, whenever I feel drained of energy, dramatically under the weather, or I find I myself stuck in a doldrum-reality-rut, I mind-full-ly remind myself to use Elwood's flip-phrase, and I instantaneously become mind-free in my present moment. I silently say, "Do not see your feet," and quick as a light switch, my chin goes up, my shoulders go back, and with a readily recharged, clearly confident, and enlightened energy, I stand up straight. Since I grew up with a very noticeable, "inferiority stoop," this simple change in posture always makes a world of difference! So the bottom line truth of this story is, if you want your life's point of view to be, "Things are looking up," *then literally look up!*

Good. Now before you go to the next section, let us once again see where you are at, and recognize how far you have come. Let us review the four stages of self-improvement you have so smartly and successfully traversed.

Exercise 7 - Stage Review: Where are You in The Planet's Population?

Comatose vs. Conscious: This is where seventy percent of the population exists.

Asleep vs. Awake: This is where thirty percent of the population lives.

Aware vs. Alive: Here is the bridge between human being versus human doing.

Mind-Full vs. Mind-Free: Here is where you live the life moments of a human doing.

Now that you know where you are in your life's character improvement, it is time to focus and pay attention.

Focus and Pay Attention!

In *Sister Act II: Back in the Habit,* Whoopi Goldberg's character Deloris says, "If you want to be somebody, if you want to go somewhere, you've got to wake up and pay attention." To this I say, "Amen." And actress Lily Tomlin once said, "I always wanted to be somebody. I should have been more specific." These two statements show how vitally important it is for us to focus and pay attention.

Let me explain why you need to focus and pay attention by using different states of energy. You may have heard the phrase, "You've got great potential. All you need to do is concentrate, focus, and pay attention." Remember how important it is for an actor or actress to be in the moment. Think of this as a similar situation. If you think of concentration, focus, and attention, as currency/*current-cy*, in-the-now energies, then you can use them to *pay* for your life. This way you will efficiently turn simple, stationary, *potential* energy, into positive, productive, *kinetic* energy. For example, American aviator Amelia Earhart once soulfully said, "Courage is the price life exacts for granting peace." Courage is a type of *focused* energy. Clearly Ms. Earhart, who was the first female aviator to fly solo across the Atlantic Ocean and went missing during her attempt to fly around the world, experienced extreme expenditures of courage in order to pay the price for her idea of a peaceful, productive life. So the next time someone tells you to, "Focus and pay attention," do it with the idea in mind that you are *buying* your next presentized life moment.

Exercise 8 - Four Focus Factors (FF) and Their Corresponding Enhanced Concentration Technique (ECT)

FF 1 - Proper Sleep | ECT 1 - Power Naps

Whether you are a morning person or a night owl, either way, you need to get the proper amount of uninterrupted sleep, which is appropriate for your life, occupations, and age. Fifteen to twenty minute power naps can be used when necessity dictates, but if you find yourself overindulging in this practice, then change your sleep schedule, and keep the naps only as a luxury, and not as a standard, normal mode of operation.

FF 2 - Diet and Exercise | ECT 2 - Miniature Behavior Modifications

It doesn't take an advanced degree in health and nutrition to know your diet and the amount of regular exercise you get does in fact directly influence your energy level. However, if you do choose to be unconscious of your diet and exercise habits, you can choose to at least do miniature behavior modifications. These include eating fruit and vegetable snacks and, whenever possible, walking and biking for transportation.

FF 3 - External Environment | ECT 3 - User-Friendly Modifications

This means limiting potential distractions and setting yourself up to succeed. For example, if there are any loud noises or music playing that keeps you from your focus, find a way to muffle the sound or shut it off completely. Or, if you need more light or special materials, set up and get what you need *before* you start working. Warning: Do not go overboard! Do not let your set-up and prep-work become a means of non-productive procrastination.

FF 4 - Internal Learning Style | ECT 4 - Self-Awareness Modifications

We all learn differently. Some are visual learners. They simply need to read the text, and they know the material. Others must use a more hands-on, "learn by doing" approach. Some are auditory learners. All they have to do is hear the information, and they learn. Most people are a combination of all three styles. Also, we all have different interests. If you find a subject interesting, you are far more likely to learn about it. When you are aware of how and what you learn best, it is much easier to modify situations and efficiently enhance your ability to concentrate, a.k.a. focus and pay attention.

And, now that you know these tips, the hope of this exercise is for you to implement the information into your daily life and ultimately be that much closer to becoming the *new and improved*, self-helped version of you. And speaking of help....

Help: Earn It!

For a long time, I did not know how to start writing this section. I stared at the computer until it finally just went to sleep. Apparently, if you have a prolonged case of in-activity-itis, and the computer gets bored with you, it does this automatically. Only this time, just to add insult to injury, I was so delusional in my writer's block, for a moment, I actually thought I heard the computer snoring!

Then, the irony brick hit me hard in the head and abruptly brought me back into focus: Help! I could ask someone for help. After all, that is what this whole section is all about. So, I did the *Who Wants to be a Millionaire?* thing, and I used a lifeline to phone-a-friend.

She answered my call and responded above and beyond all my high hopes. Only after a few minutes of describing my writing woes, she simply said, "What's the first thing that comes to mind when you hear the word help?" Naturally, having recently completed Emergency Medical Technician (EMT) certification, I said, "The Beatles!" She said, "Good. Now that you have got yourself started just keep going."

In the interest of time, I will not list all my initial ideas. However, I will say, with the cost of long-distance phone calls being what they were back in the day, and knowing how the phone companies used some form of corporate, fiscal math, which was specifically designed to make huge profits, I am sure I will be paying for that phone call, long into the next decade.

My best idea came to me as the following realization: *We are all constantly giving and receiving help. We simply semantically call it something else.* For example, every job or career everywhere, is in some shape or form, directly or indirectly, helping someone or something. But for some reason we put these occupations in other categories or describe them all with other titles and headings (i.e., Product Production or Customer Service).

The bottom line is, all these categories, titles, and headings are simply other words, which all mean occupations that help.

Another great idea was: maybe I am preaching to the choir—after all, I am writing a self-help book. Maybe you, the reader of this particular self-help book (good choice by the way), already know how to find helpful resources for yourself. Maybe the real challenge is only when you need to actually ask for help beyond yourself. I am sure most people would agree, it is much easier to ask—or to read on your own—an inanimate, self-help book, than it is to overcome your fears and ask for help from another real person, face-to-face, up-close and personal. So, whenever I am faced with the difficulty of the second idea, I consciously use the first idea's main point, to logically reason myself through the following Three Premises and Three Results exercise:

Exercise 9 - Mindset to Easily Ask for Help: Three Premises and Three Results

Three Premises:

Premise 1: Everything I do helps someone or something. This includes me.

Premise 2: Everyone is constantly giving or receiving help.

Premise 3: When I receive help, it means in some shape or form, I have *already* asked for the help.

Three Results:

Result 1: When I realize I need to ask for help, I recognize I have already accomplished a lifetime of practice.

Result 2: I am considerably more confident in my ability to ask for help, and it is infinitely easier to perform.

Result 3: I am markedly more productive and successful in my life.

I know this is true, because as soon as I implemented the Three Premises and Three Results mindset, I realized I am now receiving substantially a lot more help, which is significantly more specific to my needs and wants. *After all, I did ask for it!*

Note: I hope you will assimilate these three premises into your daily life. And I equally hope you will subsequently also achieve the same dramatic results. I also hope, whenever you do receive help, you will recognize how you absolutely always need to ultimately earn it. I became aware of this concept from the movie *Saving Private Ryan*. Near the end, Captain Miller (Tom Hanks) tells Private Ryan (Matt Damon), "Earn this. Earn it." Captain Miller is referring to the soldiers' noble acts of risking or losing their lives while on their mission to help save him, and subsequently send him home. Ryan has been given the penultimate act of help. Ryan's life has been saved. In short, Captain Miller is telling Private Ryan to do something productive with his civilian life, and thus earn and honor the help he has been given in his military life. I believe you need to follow this same code of honor in your life.

When someone or something helps you, it is your moral responsibility to do something productive with the gift. Choose to never take altruistic acts for granted. Consider it part of your religious practice, a facet of your spiritual self, or simply a foundational part of your personal code of karma. No matter what you call it, always do what needs to be done. Make a hard-held, unwavering, lifetime character commitment. Solemnly say, "I will always, absolutely, abundantly, and ultimately earn, all the holistic help I am ever gratefully given!"

Okay, you have traversed four stages of self-improvement. You know why it is important to focus and pay attention. You have learned how to easily ask for help. When you receive help, you have made a conscious character commitment to always earn it. And after a quick post view, you will move forward to Chapter 3 and you will clearly and completely See the Scene.

Post View

If you have access to the movie soundtrack for *2001: A Space Odyssey* play it! For with the completion of Chapter 2 you are now a conscious, awake, alive, mind-full, and mind-free self-improved human doing. Along with this grand evolutionary achievement, you have also successfully acquired a new, higher level of thinking. You now know why it is so imperatively important to focus and pay attention. Not only do you understand how you are constantly giving help, but from now on, whenever you receive help, you are also able to recognize and honor the fact that it is your karmic and moral duty to always, absolutely, abundantly, and ultimately earn it.

For a moment, look back with self-admiration. You have completed these six sections:

- Comatose vs. Conscious
- Asleep vs. Awake
- Aware vs. Alive
- Mind-Full vs. Mind-Free
- Focus and Pay Attention!
- Help: Earn It!

And you have completed the following four exercises:

- Comatose vs. Conscious: Clear Comparisons
- Stage Review: Where Are You in The Planet's Population?
- Four Focus Factors (FF) and Their Corresponding Enhanced Concentration Technique (ECT)
- Mindset to Easily Ask for Help: Three Premises and Three Results

You have also completed two more of The 16 Secrets of Success:

5. Focus and pay attention.

   You have complete control of your current-cy, in the now energies, and you know how to use them to pay for your life. You know how to turn simple, potential energy into positive and productive kinetic energy. You know how to easily buy presentized life moments. And you also know four focus factors and their corresponding enhance concentration techniques. You are now an expert on how to focus and pay attention.

6. Ask for help. Gratefully accept help. Earn all the help you are given.

   Now you know you are constantly giving and receiving help, and you have the mindset to easily ask for help in the future. And now you know, and will honor the code of whenever you receive help, you will always, absolutely, abundantly, and ultimately, earn it!

You have done all these things successfully! *YOU GO! YOU ARE THE CHARACTER!* Okay. Now turn the page. Our journey continues in Chapter 3: See the Scene!

CHAPTER 3:
SEE THE SCENE!

Preview

All right! Action! Scene 3! This chapter is all about what it means for a character to See the Scene! The following concepts can all be applied to fictional characterizations, but because you are a real, non-fictional character, who lives in the real world, and is in search of some real self-help, I am only going to present these concepts using real life applications. In this chapter, you will answer several questions on sight—*specialized sight.* These questions include:

- Is hindsight twenty-twenty, or can we see the past however or in whatever way we want to see it?

- Since you have already projected forward with creative visualization and goal setting, are there any other types of foresight you can use to your advantage?

- What is now-sight, and how can it be used productively?

- What should you look for and how should you use insight in your daily life?

- What is the difference between sex and holistic intimacy, (in-to- me-you-see), and what does the word BEAUTIFUL really mean?

In the last section, you will see what happens when you consciously use all these specialized sights simultaneously. You will literally learn life lessons and you will cognitively conclude school is always in session.

Hindsight

Some say hindsight is twenty-twenty, but I do not believe it is remotely that clear. Three reasons are as follows: First, if you ask any law enforcement agent, they will tell you how even the most recent of eyewitness accounts is potentially unreliable. Second, hindsight is highly susceptible to the phone game phenomenon. This means the more times you try to recall and tell a story, the more opportunities there are for the facts to be embellished, or to be completely altered altogether. Third, the more time that transpires, the more past events fade out of focus. In other words, the older you get, the higher the quantity of stories you have to recall, and it is nature's sick sense of humor to ensure you have a lower quality of mental memory with which to retain all your relevant recollections.

Another way hindsight can be entirely inaccurate is in the writing of world history. Most honest historians will admit, "History is recalled, recorded, and rewritten by the winners!" For example, the story of *How the West was Won* would have been dramatically different if it had been told by Native Americans. For a fantastic, fictional, and dramatic depiction of this thought, see the movie *Dances with Wolves*. Or, if you want to see the most recent retelling of this certainly controversial classic movie theme, see the movie *Avatar*.

In this same spirit, when we remember and retell our own story, it is only natural to paint ourselves in the best of all possible lights. In short, our own memory and storytelling talents can be boundlessly biased. Now you are probably wondering, "What does all this mean for me? How does it facilitate my self-help process?" These are good questions. With a little patience on your part, I will show you how these interesting ideas absolutely do apply to you and your new and improved, presentized self.

Here is how to use hindsight to your advantage: when you find yourself looking back, reliving past mistakes, holding on to old, ultimately unhealthy, totally toxic emotional baggage, or you are recalling unresolved regrets, remember how holistically wrong hindsight can be. Then, reset your present-day point of view. Yes, it is true. You can not change actual, factual history. But you can change and choose to see your past experiences differently. And subsequently, you can change, and choose your present-day feelings. If you forgive yourself, learn from your mistakes, and let go of all your bulky baggage, I do believe you will find, you *now* feel extremely enlightened. And *now* you are infinitely improved, and appropriately prepared, to deal with any and all present day dilemmas. And before you look forward to the next section, do the following exercise:

Exercise 10 - Hindsight: A Special Task of Past Detoxification

Step 1: Choose a past experience and write the story of that experience.

Step 2: Reset to your present point of view.

Step 3: Rewrite your past experience story as it is presently seen through your new eyes of self-forgiveness and self-enlightened hindsight.

Step 4: Repeat as often as you see a need, with as many memories as you need to review through new eyes and a new perspective.

Foresight

You have already used creative visualization to set some of your life goals. This is a classic form of foresight. It is universally used throughout countless occupations and it can be highly effective and successful in guiding your trajectory. For example, Robin Williams spent most of his childhood creating character voices and imaginary friends. In his mind's eye, he saw himself using these talents to become a successful comedian and dramatic actor. I think we can all agree he was a very clear visionary. Also in the movie magic world, creative visualization provides all the inspiration for every special effect. Now you are probably saying to yourself, "Okay. Been there. Done that. I get it. Tell me something I don't know or I haven't already used." Okay, here goes.

Another form of foresight is scenario selection. This is a series of predictions. First, you think, "If I say or do X what will be the possible repercussions or results?" Then, when you've predicted enough possible scenarios, you make a choice. You decide where you want to go with the dialogue or action. Actors and actresses often use this technique in improvisation games and during the rehearsal process. It is also very helpful when you're experimenting with script interpretations and developing specific character traits.

In the real world, using this technique can be literally vital to an actor or actress' health and well-being. For example, when making a movie, the stunt coordinator must constantly take into account safety risk management. The coordinator must accurately predict if the ends (getting the shot), justify the means (how the stunt is done). After all, real lives are on the line.

In summary, scenario selection foresight is a principal part of any real-world decision-making process. Granted, the time you invest in it will greatly depend on the importance of the decision being made, but still it is universally used in *all* decisions. And the sooner you are able to efficiently use it in your daily life, the more self-empowered you will be, and the easier it will be for you to foresee your own super successful, fantastic future.

Now-Sight

In past chapter sections, you have learned how important it is for an actor or actress to *be in the moment* and *act now*, and how you must consciously *presentize yourself.* Now-sight is a more all-encompassing, holistic concept than these simple theater terms. Now-sight is *knowing* where your character currently is in the grand scheme of your life.

A past, prime sports example was Michael Jordan. Every time he retired and came back, it was clear he knew exactly where he was in his basketball career and in his life. After winning the first Chicago Bulls three-peat NBA Championships, he retired at the top of his game. Then, with his father's death and his baseball interests processed and pursued, he came back to his true north: Basketball! He came back *For the Love of the Game!* This is the title of his autobiography and newspaper headlines *around the world,* read in large, bold print, **"HE'S BACK!"** And then after *the second* of his three-peat NBA Championship runs, he retired again with nothing left to prove. He only came back again when the team for which he was part owner, The Carolina Wizards, needed him to show them how to play the game at its highest level. He did his best with flashes of brilliance. The team doubled their wins from the previous year, but ultimately, in the end, he knew he was too old to play anymore and he would never be able to par his past performances, so he respectfully retired permanently.

Now-sight is most productive when it is used as a self-assessment tool. The key is to use it at periodic, set intervals in your life. Examples include yearly check-ups, five-year benchmarks, and ten-year class reunions. When now-sight is used within these time frames, it gives you the opportunity to do noteworthy, self-progress reports. These will help you bring your life into focus, and will help you avoid blindly living on cruise-control. You will be able to see how you are staying on course and how you are still on the right heading for achieving all your creatively visualized life goals.

BEAUTIFUL Insight

Most people recognize what it means when someone says, "You are very insightful about (insert the external subject of the day)," but when insight is turned internally they often claim situational blindness. This is because most people do not know what they are insight-fully seeing. Even if they do have some small clue, they do not know how to use what they see as helpful tools in their daily lives. The key is to think of insight as not only simply seeing inside your heart, but also as healthfully hearing inside your head.

Use the following checklist and do your own insight self-inventory:

___ **Insight Item:** Inner Conscience

Insight Identification: Everyone has this/these voice(s) inside their head, which helps determine wrong from right. Some see it as the classic cartoon battle between the little devil and the little angel, but I believe everyone has this internal voice in some form or another. Even Pinocchio had Jiminy Cricket, and Pinocchio was just a small wooden puppet with wanna-be-human issues. So, whenever you hear your Inner Conscience, turn the volume up on the side of right.

___ **Insight Item:** Inner Critic

Insight Identification: This is the all-negative voice who, "argues for your limitations." (Richard Bach *Illusions*) It points out everything you can not do and in great detail tells you why, "Your dreams are impossible!" It persuades you to quit before you even start, or sadly, just before you are about to fantastically finish. It is the voice that says "NO!" to all your "What ifs?" So do yourself a favor, for this voice, turn the volume down or off.

___ **Insight Item:** Inner Champion

Insight Identification: Hopefully, this voice is louder than your Inner Critic because it is the champion of all your good causes. It is your very own personal, enthusiastic, impassioned cheerleader, who pulls for you from the sidelines of your mind. It is Wilson Phillips singing "Hold On!" And followed by Queen's "We Are The Champions!" It reminds you how perseverance is the mother of success.

___ **Insight Item:** Inner Child

Insight Identification: Just like a real child, you must nurture this inner voice. You must listen to it and give it love and understanding. You must let it know it is safe to speak your mind. And more often than not, when it wants you to be playful, Just Do It.

___ **Insight Item:** Inner Highest, Best Self

Insight Identification: This is your voice of reason. This voice holds you to your highest code of honor, ethics, scruples, and morals. Make yourself a promise: my inner highest, best self, will always be my final answer. It will always get my last word.

___ **Insight Item:** Inner Integrity

Insight Identification: When people take the time to look at you and attempt to read your character, make sure you're an open book. Be honest and true; never be two-faced.

Make sure your internal self matches your external show. Or in other words, make sure what they see is what they get.

When you pull all these together, the key to having and using insight in your daily life is to listen and health-fully hear. You need to turn down the volume on your Inner Critic and turn up the volume on your Inner Champion. You need to cater to the small, soft voice of your Inner Child and every day set aside quality playtime. You need to hear both sides of your Inner Conscience and let your final decisions on what to do, be made by your Inner Highest, Best Self. You need to make this action choice be your *Who Wants to be a Millionaire?* final answer. And when you listen every time, and you follow all these points, that is when you will be using all your powers of insight to their highest degree of efficiency and positive personal productivity.

Another insight concept asks the question, "What does the word BEAUTIFUL real-ly mean?" The answer is an internal thing. Pretty and handsome people are overtly obvious. But truly BEAUTIFUL people are more covertly created. I will explain. BEAUTIFUL *real-ly* means, the ability to Be (yourself,) Enlightened, Alive, Unique, Trustworthy, Intelligent, Faithful, and Unconditionally Loving. And if you consciously choose to acquire all these character traits, you will be infinitely better equipped, to one day, in the eyes of another equally beautiful beholder, to holistically become, a real-ly beautifully beheld.

Holistic Intimacy and The Hierarchy of Human Sexuality

Intimacy (in-to-me-you-see) is the most personal part of anyone's life. Because it is not just about how closely you relate to others, in day-to-day relationships, but it also refers to one's lifetime of sexuality. This can be a sensitive subject. Because it also shows how our most intimate thoughts and feelings affect our interactions with the outside world.

And now, "Let's Talk About Sex!" What is the difference between sex and holistic intimacy? The best way to answer this question is to understand the hierarchy of human sexuality. Note: It needs to be said. I am not a sex therapist or professional psychologist. But, in the immortal words of Forrest Gump, *I believe I am a smart man, and,* "I know what love is." This is what I know.

Basic Self-Gratification: This is a healthy act. Mental fantasy and/or activity aides can be used, but not always chosen or necessary. The key to this definition is how only one person does this act with his or her own body.

Advanced Self-Gratification: This is an act or acts, which is/are done by more than one person. The key to this definition is there are no emotional investments. It is people just "getting off" or "having sex." Taking all safe-sex concerns and practices into account, this can also be a healthy act. *But only if everyone knows what is being done!* If anyone does not know, then he/she/they will most likely be emotionally, and/or even physically, hurt.

Courtship: This is where two people start getting to know each other. They have feelings, emotional investments, for/in each other. This unset period of time usually includes an indeterminate number of very specialized acts. Examples of these acts are hanging out together, alone as a couple and/or in various types of social settings, and going out on dates. The key to the definition of courting is that the two people are beginning to learn about the whole-self of the person they are spending time with, and at the same time, themselves. People at this time are not just experiencing each other's body parts, but ideally, they are also learning the ins and outs of *the whole holistic person(s)*.

Foreplay: These are specifically sensual/sexual acts. These two people know each other very well, and they both verbally claim they are, "in a relationship." This is everything which leads to orgasms. Yes. EVERYTHING! And I say, "Do not live for *only* orgasms. Live for a lifetime of for(e)play!"

Make LOVE! (Lots Of Vulnerable Emotions! Lots Of Vibrant Energies!): This is when both people honestly, openly, and real-ly put their hearts on the line. A slightly subtle and also a substantially sensible point to remember here is, "You never make love *to* a person, you always make love *with* a person." Both people must genuinely care about each other to make it work. The bad news is yes, it can be a lot of work. The good news is also yes, when you do make the effort and actually do the work, the payoff is priceless.

Holistic Intimacy: All the sights so far—hindsight, foresight, now-sight, insight—have been internal. The origin of the sight of intimacy—seeing into someone else and allowing them to see into you—is external. It transpires when someone knows you better than you know yourself. It is a key part of the highest and deepest level of The Hierarchy of Human Sexuality, and it can be achieved in all types of relationships. For example, this specialized sight also applies when parents know their children or when best friends know everything about one another. So, if you are incredibly fortunate, and able to find your holistic intimacy soulmate(s), or if they are able to find you, then this is when your life will become the best of all possible worlds. You will realize there is really nothing more valuable on this planet, than sharing real holistic intimacy.

I will quickly end this section with two more thoughts: First, Oscar Wilde rightly said, "If you fall in love with yourself, you will begin a lifelong romance." Self-love, intuitive integrity, and a personal code of honor, *once you have them, they are yours for life*.

Second, Ralph Waldo Emerson so eloquently wrote, "What lies behind us, and what lies before us, are tiny matters when compared to what lies within us." In other words, what we see in hindsight and foresight are slight, when they are compared with what we see with insight. This is what happens when we are in relationships of holistic intimacy.

WARNING!

Abuse and rape are not sexual acts!

They are different forms of control, power, assault, and violence!

Please, no matter what your age, if you are, or if you suspect you are, a present, and/or a past, victim of either one of these two types of illegal acts, then you need to immediately report it to the proper authorities. You need to get personal and professional help and support. Contact and connect with the best people, who will help you process all your short and long term, minor and major, issues and concerns.

This is a matter of life and health!

Learn Life Lessons: School is Always in Session!

The last section in this chapter is a reminder of a few important life lessons. Its purpose is to encourage you to consistently strive to be a lifelong learner. After all, school is always in session!

Life Lesson 1: See through new paradigms and think outside the box. Use these two challenges to test your vision.

Challenge 1:

Without lifting your pen connect all nine dots with only four straight lines.

```
●   ●   ●


●   ●   ●


●   ●   ●
```

Challenge 2:

What does this set of letters represent? HIJKLMNO

Challenge 1 Answer:

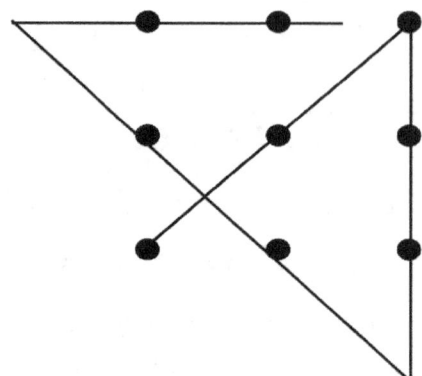

Challenge 2 Answer:

HIJKLMNO: This set of letters is, "H to O" in the English alphabet. But, in the paradigm of science, we all know, H_2O represents water.

Now, I realize these two challenges are just the proverbial tip-of-the-iceberg when it comes to giving examples of how to see through new paradigms and think outside the box, but I do hope you see the idea. Finding ways to exercise our brain and our perceptions of reality, help our brains stay young and elastic. Because if you truly want to become a new and improved, creative character then learning this life lesson is extremely essential.

Life Lesson 2: Pain vs. Suffering

I learned this life lesson from the M. Kathleen Casey quote, "Pain is inevitable, suffering is optional." In typical dramatic form, this idea foreshadows Chapter 5 in the section on attitude. In this case, I feel it is important enough to tip my hand. So, here's my advice. *Learn now! Attitude is everything!*

Life Lesson 3: What doesn't kill you makes you stronger

This life lesson is practically synonymous with Pain vs. Suffering. I include it here, both for its own merit, and so you can see how it is perfectly legal and totally normal to experience different versions of life lessons until they are completely learned. For only when a life lesson is tangibly learned, and real-ly used, will you actually have the ability to move forward with your life's education. Remember, school is always in session! Be a lifelong learner!

Life Lesson 4: Yes, please

In 1992 I was an enthusiastic exchange student, stationed in Sheffield, England. It was an amazing learning experience, and an absolutely fabulous, fun-filled adventure of a lifetime. While I was there, I learned countless life lessons, and one in particular has been unbelievably useful: Some people like to play host. They feel better when they believe you feel completely comfortable in their casual company. So, when someone offers you a drink, a cup of tea perhaps, you should consciously consider helping the person by gratefully accepting it. This way, they feel good about you and about themselves for being of value to you. In other words, no matter how unthirsty you may be, you should always accept the drink. In short, say, "Yes please."

WARNING!

To anyone under the legal drinking age: Due to countless legal, health, and personal safety concerns, you need to remember alcoholic drinks are clearly an exception to this life lesson. Hopefully, you will never have to learn this life lesson the hard way. So use good judgment in expressing any personal limitations around alcohol.

The key to learning life lessons is to use all of your specialized sights simultaneously and see the scene in complete context as your life unfolds before your eyes. Use your hindsight to review and see what you have learned from your past, "mistakes." Miles Davis said, "Do not fear mistakes—there are none." The way I see it, there are only learning opportunities. Use your foresight to project what you have learned into your future, new and improved, and smarter self. Use your now-sight to see where your new life knowledge fits into the big picture of your new, presentized self. And finally, tell all your insight and inner voices you have learned something new. Make it your life's practice to use all this new knowledge in all your future self's inner deliberations.

Okay. Now you See the Scene! Your eyes are wide open. As the song, "I Can See Clearly Now" says, when the rain is gone, you can see all obstacles and all rainbows. You can know that what is coming is going to be a clear and bright, sun-shiny day. And with that in mind, (and after a quick post view,) you can begin and you can Set the Stage! You will know, your future, new and improved, self-helped, holistic life-character, is almost ready to be royally revealed!

Post View

In the movie *The Abyss*, deep sea diver Lindsey Brigman desperately tries to explain how *what* we see can be dramatically influenced by *how* we see. She says, "We all see what we want to see. … You have to look with better eyes." In Chapter 3, you have learned how to see holistically. Your eyesight is now crystal-clear, bright, and positive. In short, you are a new and improved, victorious visionary!

For a moment, look back with self-admiration.

You have completed the following six sections:

- Hindsight
- Foresight
- Now-Sight
- BEAUTIFUL Insight
- Holistic Intimacy and The Hierarchy of Human Sexuality
- Learn Life Lessons: School is Always in Session!

You have also read through and completed the following four items:

- Hindsight: A Special Task of Past Detoxification
- Insight Inventory
- The Hierarchy of Human Sexuality
- Two Life Lesson Challenges

And you have completed three more of The 16 Secrets of Success:

7. How you think is everything. Eliminate negatives. Think only positives.
8. Be a lifelong learner.
9. Learn to see and analyze all of life's little details. Learn from your mistakes. Follow the flow until all life lessons are learned.

You have completed these three secrets of success by learning how to incorporate all four specialized sights simultaneously, and by efficiently processing all the points made from the final section, Learn Life Lessons: School is Always in Session! If you wish to delve deeper into special solo soul-searching journeys, do some research on Aboriginal walkabouts and Native American vision quests. I also highly recommend the movie *Vision Quest*.

Congratulations! You have done all these things successfully! *YOU GO! YOU ARE THE CHARACTER!* Okay. Now turn the page. Our journey continues in Chapter 4: Set the Stage!

CHAPTER 4:
SET THE STAGE!

Preview

All right! Action! Scene 4! Chapter 3 was about finding your place in the big picture and learning how to use specialized sights to clearly See the Scene! Chapter 4 will show you how to Set the Stage! First, you will SORT (Self, Occupations, Relationships, and Time Transitions) your life into a four-file system. You will learn time management skills and you will efficiently organize the life character you have so fantastically formed. Second, you will learn the difference between simply feeling lonely versus only being alone. Third, you will understand the need, when you search for lifetime role models, to create MAGIC (Make A Good Intelligent Choice), and to sail the seven Cs (Collect Cool Companions and Consciously Choose them with Clear Criteria). And finally fourth, you will set your mindset and you will become a whole-world, whole-humanity, global thinker. You will *know* a fundamental truth: you create your own reality. And fact *and* fiction: It takes all kinds to make a world.

SORT Your Life Into A Four-File System

This section parallels Chapter 1, Part Two: Fact Foundation PIES Chart. The main difference is, instead of focusing on *individual* character, we will focus on *social* character. Here is the origin story of my four-file system. I have a big brother. He is two years older and seven inches taller. He has always been tall. In fourth grade he was a towering, five-foot-tall Snoopy, in *You're a Good Man, Charlie Brown*. Compared to his classmates, he looked more like a Great Dane than a Beagle. But anyway, when it comes to some of our brother-to-brother character traits, we are as different as night and day and we most definitely do not see things eye to eye. A past, prime example, was our adolescent, bedroom organizational styles. My room was OCD clean, but his room was a tornado town's ground zero! But I did discover, despite the disaster zone of debris, there was in fact a method to his mad-mess.

One day I pushed aside a pile of papers, which were blocking the door, and I walked into my brother's room. I gave voice to my thoughts and said, "How can you possibly find anything in all this chaotic clutter?" He countered with a challenge. "Okay. A buck an item. You name it. I will tell you where it is. Is it a bet?" I thought, "There is no way. This is easy money." So I said, "Sure. Right. Okay. It's a bet."

I looked around. Wow! At first, I could not distinguish any specific, single item. Then I saw it. The corner of his wallet was barely visible, under a large pile of laundry, wedged between the bed and bureau. "Wallet." I said. "Floor." He answered. After a *long* pause, I reluctantly realized *it was to be his only answer*. You see, I *assumed* he was going to give me a little more detail on the *exact* location of the wallet. But as he was, and still is, my big brother, I suddenly understood how he did in fact have an organizational paradigm. The dramatic difference between his system and mine? His categories were bigger! Bed. Desk. Closet. Floor. He only had four big categories to worry about. It was beyond brilliant! So I handed him a dollar. I quit while I was behind. But, because of what I learned that day, I do feel it was one of the best bucks I have ever spent. The seeds of the four-file system were planted in my mind.

So here it is. This is my four-file system. To improve your time-management skills, and to organize your life character, SORT your world into the following four big categories:

Self: Give yourself permission to be un-social. Solo time is vital.

Occupations: Find your vocation and feel like you are on a virtual vacation.

Relationships: For all kinds, consult The ABCs Of a Successful Relationship.

Time-Transitions: Set your pulse pace. Set your rhythm of life. Put everything together and holistically compose yourself.

For further explanation, read the following four sub-sections.

Note: Make and keep a Noteworthy Notes Right Results file for each big category.

Self

In her brilliant bestselling book *The Artist's Way*, Julia Cameron talks about how we should take ourselves on artist dates. This is a special, self-love experience, and a sensational self-health, private practice. Think of it as setting aside quality, personal time on purpose. The primary reason for scheduling these solitary activities is to refill your creative energy well. The key is to highly honor and value yourself, and for you to graciously give yourself permission to be positively and productively un-social.

My version of this concept is to make Self be the first of my big four files. My term of choice is solo time. If you wish to have a balanced, healthy life, you need to give yourself permission to confidently claim this time. I believe this is vital! Think of yourself as an airplane pilot who is celebrating your freedom and finally flying solo.

After hearing this analogy, people often ask me, "What are acceptable activities I can do?" My response is always the same. I simply smile and say, "Well flyer, you are the pilot. The sky's the limit." After hearing this, if they are still in a confused state of paralysis by analysis, I tell them what works for me. I tell them I make jewelry. This is adult LEGOs®. Or I go to coffee shops to do creative writing and journaling. This is where I wrote some of my best *Andrewisms* poetry, and where I wrote and edited the majority of my books. Or I do low exertion exercising, i.e., stretching, walking, minimalist-movings, or yoga. Or I listen to music. Or I read. Or I do bookstore browsing. Or I do one of the most powerful, peaceful, and popular of all positive pastimes: I detox and dissolve all the day's stresses and worries away, when I do self-guided meditation.

Self-guided meditation is a very personal activity. It can simply be silently centering yourself and doing basic creative visualization. Or it can be highly ritualistic and involve a variety of instrumental music selections, nature sounds, chanting, candles, and/or aromatherapy. The amount of time one gives to the practice is also unique to the individual practitioner. As it is with so many personal and private practices, the key to doing it "right," is to commit to being consistent, and to always do whatever works for you.

In the theater world, self-guided meditation is commonly used in ensemble bonding exercises, individual pre-production warm-ups, and for diffusing, transforming, and transposing stage fright. To put this idea in practice, a diligent director once gave me a great piece of pre-acting advice. He said, "To cure the butterflies in your stomach, use a quick, five-minute mini-meditation and focus all your emotional energy directly into your play-full performance. In short, get your belly's butterflies to fly in formation."

Pre-Exercise Note: One of the most commonly overlooked concepts which is vital to ensuring solo time be healthy, beneficial, productive, and successful, is the need for you to create a sacred space. This physical location can be absolutely anywhere *you* choose. The point is, no matter where you set it, make yourself a commitment contract to keep it private. In short, make sure you are the only one using it for your own special solo time.

Use solo time and self-guided meditation to do the following exercise:

Exercise 11 - Daily-Debriefing: A Present Detoxification Process

Step 1: Debrief and Discard - Clear your mind and eliminate all negative thoughts. See yourself as a computer. Mentally clear away all clutter from your desktop.

Step 2: Rewire and Reprogram - Transpose all negative thoughts to positive affirmations.

Step 3: Review and Reset - See life from your new point of view and confirm it.

Step 4: Hard-Wire - Daily confirmation develops an energy efficient, positively productive hard-drive.

For further clarification, read *Meditations and Creative Visualization* by Shakti Gawain.

Note to parents: One of the best things you can do to nurture, support, and legitimately love your children is to respect their space. Of course, if their space is in your space, i.e., your home, then there definitely needs to be some communicated explanations of your rules and expectations. However, in general, if you respect your children's privacy, they are much more likely to invite you in their space, in their lives, and on their terms.

Note to teens: One of the best things you can do to enhance, strengthen, and dramatically improve your relationship with your parents or guardians is to, as much as possible, appreciate and be genuinely grateful for the job(s) they are performing. As best you can, see if you can understand and empathize with their motivations for saying and doing the things they say and do. When your parents do communicate and explain their rules and expectations, make sure you give them the benefit of the doubt. Always remember: you are both on the same side. Think of it as you are all Love-A-Lotly on Team-Teen!

Occupations

Your most valuable commodity is time. There are only 168 hours in a week. The key question in this subsection is, "How do you occupy your time?"

I am including an exercise that will help you determine your answer.

Exercise 12 - Plot A Week's Worth of Spending: Create a Color-Coded Time Occupations Bar Graph

1) How many hours a week do you spend sleeping?   _____
   Include all power naps and bedtime.

2) How many hours a week do you spend eating?   _____
   Include all food preparation time, real meals, and small snacks.

3) How many hours a week do you spend on personal hygiene, hair   _____
   grooming/styling, using makeup/skin care, and getting *all* dressed?
   Include all bathroom time and getting ready-to-do-anything time.

4) How many hours a week do you spend working at job(s), career(s)?   _____
   Include all school, homemaker, family care, chores, and activities. Include
   all schoolwork, studying, and work-related business duties.

5) How many hours a week do you spend on technology-time?   _____
   Include all time watching TV, gaming, gadgeting, cell phone-ing, iPad-
   tableting, and e-computerizing.

6) How many hours a week do you spend exercising?   _____
   Include all formal and informal methods.

7) How many hours a week do you spend commuting?   _____
   Include all means of transportation.

8) How many hours a week do you spend on hobbies/special interests?   _____
   Include all reading, arts and crafts, recreational sports, and/or
   community/political activities.

9) How many hours a week do you spend on leisure/luxury free time?   _____
   Include all playtime, relaxation events, and any "alternative" activities.

   How many hours a week do you spend on all other time expenditures?
10) Add your own activity(s) that has/have not been already assigned.

   _____   _____

   Add all your answers.

   This number is your Total Time Spent* for a week.   _____

*If you have been totally honest with your estimates, your total time spent (TTS) will be much more than 168. Do not worry. We will talk about the reason for this result later.

Now complete this exercise and create a color-coded Time Occupations Bar Graph. Record and plot your data on the template shown below.

Hours per week / Activity	10	20	30	40	50	60	70	80	90	100	110	120
1–Sleep												
2–Meals												
3–Hygiene												
4–School/Work												
5–Tech												
6–Exercise												
7–Commuting												
8–Hobbies												
9–Free Time												
10–Other												

Choose a color to represent each category and color over to its Total Time Spent number.

If you have more than ten time occupations/activities, expand your graph as needed.

When you are done, you will tangibly see how you spend a week's worth of time. And once again, if you have been totally honest with your estimates, then your Total Time Spent will be much more than 168 hours. The reason for this result is a perfectly normal, completely natural, nature-of-the-beast phenomenon of human behavior. I'm talking about multi-tasking.

Take a look at your bar graph. Subtract all your sleep time. Suddenly you will see just how many activities you were actually attempting to do, in such a short amount of time. And you will also see how it is no wonder you were so susceptible to stress, and why you had so much trouble focusing and paying attention.

Now you know exactly how you spend your time. And knowing is half the battle. Now you can consciously use your newly created self-help resources. You can review and apply the four focus factors you learned in Chapter 2. When you need to reassure yourself on how you are newly and truly being cost-efficient with the way you spend your time, simply redo this exercise. Create a new and presentized, color-coded Time Occupations Bar Graph. Every time you complete the exercise, save the results in your Fact Foundation File. Cover up the old version with the new one and keep track of your productivity and progress.

Four Quotes and Four Points

Here are a few quotes, which illustrate the final four points of this subsection.

First, George Burns has been quoted as saying, "Find an occupation you love, and you will never work another day in your life." This is positive multi-tasking. My advice is to set a goal. As much as possible, make work and play synonymous.

Second, Aristotle said, "Where the needs of the world and your talents cross, there lies your vocation." This is your calling. This is your true (for you) north. So find your life-path's intersection and answer the call. Find your occupational vocation and all your wonderful work will feel like a virtual vacation!

Third, Oscar Wilde said, "Nowadays people know the price of everything and the value of nothing." *Always know, money is only a tool!* Never let it become an occupational obsession. Never let it overwhelm you into being something you are not. Never value money and material merchandise more than priceless immaterial items such as family, friends, honor, and love. If you are completely miserable and you holistically hate your job, *know* that there is no amount of money in the world, which will buy you enough *true* happiness, and real-ly replace all your lost lifetime. Never make money hoarding or power-mongering your addict's addiction *drug of need!* In short, never simply settle for only making a living. *Adjust your ambition, so you no-doubt-know and you whole-heart-ly feel you are absolutely making, an amazingly abundant, aliving!* (See Chapter 2.)

Fourth, Mark Twain said, "Put all your eggs in one basket and watch that basket!" So my advice to you is, use steadfast stubbornness and poignant patience, to make sure you balance your *one*, biggest and best basket. With your whole heart, completely commit to magnificently manifesting your biggest and best dreams. Don't be a silly rabbit. Remember what Aesop's turtle fable taught us all, "Slow and steady wins the race." *Never give up! Don't quit! And always know, no matter what, you will win in the end!*

Relationships

Relationship: A significant connection between two or more people and their involvement with each other, specifically as it regards how they behave, communicate, cooperate, and feel toward each other.

The ABCs of a Successful Relationship

A: Attitude is everything! Appreciate your life and be accountable to your affirmations. It is the quality, not the quantity, of your relationships which determines your feelings of real abundance. Accept people as they are, right from the start. Never enter into any kind of relationship with the intent or desire to change or fix a person. You can not change anyone who does not want to change. Finally, being attractive is a holistic PIES situation.

The Origin Story of the "Are You Attractive?" Life Lesson

One weekend in college, I threw myself a pointless pity-party. On Thursday afternoon, I finished my last class of the week, and I went to my dorm room to be a shut-in. I was single, lonely, and completely committed to being totally miserable for the whole weekend. Three days later, early Sunday evening, I got a phone call. One of my friends was calling to see if I was enjoying the long awaited, warm weather. As soon as she heard my voice, she knew everything.

First, she reassured me I was unconditionally loved. Then, she told me to look in a mirror. After a short, dramatic pause, she said, "Have you shaved?"

I told the truth. "No."

"Okay. Have you showered?"

My complete confession continued. "No."

Her last two questions hit home. "Are you attractive? And when you look and smell the way you do, would you go out with you?"

My accurate answers were unfortunately unavoidable. "No. I guess not."

"Okay." she said. "So tonight, before bed, shower and shave. And when you wake up tomorrow, you will clearly look better and you will certainly smell better. Then, put a sweet smile on your face, go outside, and show the world all the love in your heart. Adjust your attitude! And your enlightened attractiveness will light up the world! Tomorrow is going to be a beautiful day! If you woefully wallow in self-pity, and unhappily hide in your room, not only will you miss living your life, but the whole world will miss you being your best self!" By Monday morning I had followed her intuitive instructions to the letter. I definitely did look better. I am sure I smelled better. And yes, I most emphatically felt a whole lot better!

The truth is, this awesome advice was some of the best I have ever heard in my life. For whenever I find myself feeling the way I did on that particular Thursday, I remember what my fabulous friend told me on the following Sunday. And consequently I consciously choose to feel the way I did on that magnificent Monday. In short, I refuse to be receptive to self-pity, and I will not waste any more wonderful weekends, or weekdays, of my life.

B: Recall two concepts from Chapter 3. First, manifest what it means to be real-ly BEAUTIFUL. Second, believe in your inner, highest, best self. Trust it will tell you everything you need to know to effectively make all the best choices and holistically help you lead the best life you can possibly live.

C: Consciously create consistent communications. Be sure everyone is clear about the unique roles they are playing in your life, and they all know the context of the relationship. Make and honor all commitments, and when, not if, there are tough times, use your conflict-control skills. Focus your emotions. Remain calm, cool, and collected. If you need help acquiring these special skills, and making life choices, I highly recommend hiring a couple's counselor, and/or a personal life coach. These extremely educated, uniquely talented, school-of-life trained, and career-to-personality matched professionals can enhance cooperation in all types of relationships.

D: Know your deal-breakers. These are character traits or behaviors, which either "I cannot live with…," or "I cannot live without …" For example, I cannot live with a smoker, and I cannot live without family and friends. When you encounter one of life's obtrusive obstacles, don't be discouraged. Change your disabilities into positive, productive, and different abilities. In short, deal with it. Develop your holistic self. Purposely do the day-to-day, little things, which make a big difference. Determine your destination and discover your dreams. Know what you want. Have a clear idea what you are getting yourself into. And if you do not know, then with all doable diligence, define it as soon as possible. A great movie example is *Casablanca*. Throughout the story, Rick, played by Humphrey Bogart, is constantly deciding where he stands in relation to everyone else in his café and in the wartime world. And as we all know, from his forever-famous last line, with Louie, Rick poignantly recognizes what he is getting himself into. And so he says, "This looks like the beginning of a beautiful friendship."

E: Eliminate stress and negativity. Simplify your life. Strive towards personal enlightenment. Approach life as an exploration of enriching experiences. Learn to enjoy life every day. As it is appropriate, show empathy. Do what you can to empower people with positive, productive energy. Never let your relationships become stale, stagnant, or stuck. Make sure all your relationships continue to grow and positively evolve.

F: Fully feel your feelings. When you bury negative emotions, they can cause countless short- and long-term health issues. At the same time, never take negative feelings out on other people. This can cause violent conflicts and can be extremely detrimental and disastrously dangerous! And also as you learned in the Chapter 3 Hindsight section, forgiveness is a vital ingredient in every healthy relationship.

G: Acquire an attitude of gratitude. This applies to life's challenges and its priceless gifts. Robert Louis Stevenson said, "A friend is a gift you give yourself." So, when you are given a gift, of any kind, including genetic gifts, I believe it is your karmic duty to perpetuate the cycle of "what goes around comes around." In short, acquire the positive character traits of being totally genuine and extremely generous in sharing your gifts.

H: Have a good sense of humor and a clear code of honor. Remember, more often than not, honesty is the best policy. And if you want relationships to thrive, celebrate all times of health and happiness. And to round out letter H's character traits, see the movie *Shawshank Redemption* and listen to the musical *Damn Yankees*. They tangibly tell us "Hope is a good thing. Maybe the best of things." and "You Gotta Have Heart!"

I: Primarily in romantic relationships, I see two main models of behavior. The first I represent with the symbol of a capital letter A. It happens when two people compromise or give up a part of themselves (at the top). They meet each other halfway and form a bond of the heart (in the middle). With this type of connection, two people end up, completing each other, like in the movie *Jerry Maguire*. The second I represent with the symbol of a capital letter H. It happens when two people, who are already complete, independent individuals, form a bond of the heart (in the middle). They clearly create an un-single, one-unified couple which is greater than the sum of its parts. Both models have their own set of pros and cons. I highly recommend, when you find yourself forging a newfound relationship, picking the model which inspires the most confidence for you and is inherently the most applicable and appropriate *for both* members of the partnership. Then, trust your intuition, set your intention, and strictly stick to your collective choice, with holistic honesty, and absolute integrity.

J: Do not judge unless you are ready to be judged. Eliminate jealousy. It's an unworthy waste of precious time and aliving life energy. But, if you do find yourself green with envy, remember what Kermit the Frog taught us, in one of the greatest life-lesson songs of all time. "It's Not Easy Being Green." This song showed us how to accept ourselves for who we are right now, and helped us accept all the parts we cannot change. And, as long as you have been on this self-improvement journey, you are, as the Beatles said, "Getting Better All The Time." And at all times, you are working on refining all your character traits which you can change. And may all of your relationship journeys be joyful!

54

K: Perform random acts of kindness. And if you real-ly want to help change the world, consciously choose your acts un-randomly. And as Carole A. Fletcher, my true friend, candid conscience, and workbook professional photographer extraordinaire says, "Kind words and kind actions will take you far. And wherever you go in the world, always travel with a life-code-of-loving-kindness."

L: The Beatles were right. In times of trouble due to past made mistakes, "Let It Be." And from *Frozen*, the same sentiment is said about emotional luggage, "Let It Go." And as we talked about in Chapter 3, learn life lessons. Also be sure to listen. This is perhaps the most important of all communication skills. And often cited as the number one key ingredient in any healthy relationship, you need to have lots of laughter. Another key concept comes from my parents. They say, "You need to like the company you keep. If you like them for who they are and you like who you are when you are with them, then everything else will grow naturally." My parents have been together for over sixty years. Clearly they practice what they preach. Finally, I will finish where I started: The Beatles, remind us "All You Need is Love!"

M: Make magic moments. Be demonstratively and dramatically romantic. Set aside quality time to share the truly important things in life. Be a magic mirror. Help the people you love see themselves as you do in the best of all possible lights.

N: Notice all the little details. So when changes do occur, you can share and celebrate them together. Also, always be nice.

O: Always keep an open heart and an open mind. When it comes to using the phrase, "You are my one and only." Only say it if you truly mean it.

P: Be positive, patient, playful, pleasant, and passionate. Always politely say please.

Q: Begin and end every day with a little quintessential, quiet time. To learn about people, ask questions. Conduct your life, as if you are on an admirable, honorable, noble, and unquestionably high-quality vision quest.

R: It's not enough to simply *know* right from wrong. You also have to *show* you know. Take 100% real responsibility for your life. Be accountable for your actions. Be a responsible human doing. Make it a moral imperative to efficiently exercise your ability to respond. And Aretha Franklin sing-spelled it perfectly: "Respect" is key and best when it's kept. If lost, it's hard to reestablish. And for relationships to truly work, there must be mutual respect and shared interests for fun and relaxation. A helpful tool for keeping relationships healthy is role-playing. And when you do retrospective thinking, remove all regrets. And finally remember a conflict resolution point. It is not always necessary to persistently prove you are real-ly right.

S: In all relationships, forge feelings of safety and security. Always say, "I am sincerely sorry." Make it a point of pride to create relationships which surpass all sentimental songs. Now let's see. Am I forgetting a super S word? Yes! Wow! I forgot to talk about sex. No wait. I covered that sensitive, sensual subject in Chapter 3. Silly me. And this reminds me, be silly. And in this same spirit, make sure your sarcasm is sweet, not sour.

T: This concept is for all parents and/or any individual who wears the hat of teacher. Perhaps the hardest position to take when dealing with children you are personally or professionally responsible for, is the position of providing tough love. Also, timing is everything. Phil Collins reminds us to wait when he sings "You Can't Hurry Love." It does not matter how long it takes. You have to trust the timing will be right. That was nice of him, don't you think? You should be equally thoughtful. My thinking along these lines is as follows: since you can not put love on a timeline, live for today. Carpe diem! Seize the day! Be full of life, not strife. And when it comes to living in life's flow, do not force it.

U: Create a perfect union. This is two imperfect people who complement each other perfectly. Change your thinking to the Star Trek code of Gene Roddenberry, "The needs of the many outweigh the needs of the few or the one." In short, for all your choices, think first in terms of, "How will this decision ultimately affect us?"

V: Chapter 3 was all about specialized sights. So it stands to reason I would see positive vision as a fundamental tool for establishing healthy and successful relationships. Remember the line from *The Abyss*, "You have to look with better eyes …." Once you see better, you need to subsequently speak and listen better. With invigorated vitality, find your voice. And with enhanced interest, heighten your hearing, and holistically heed the advice from the Christian Slater movie title, *Pump Up the Volume!*

W: Jack Canfield tells us, "You can't hire someone else to do your push-ups for you." To be a success you have to do your own work. In all types of relationships you have to make the effort to put yourself out there and at least meet people halfway. You need to establish a model of efficient teamwork. And you need to welcome warmth. Some examples include affection quickies, mutual massages, routinely scheduled snuggle times, shared showers, holds and hugs, positive pillow talk, and for no particular reason at all, willing, wanted, wonderful royal romance and self-initiated intimacy.

X: Make Xs (kisses) customary. Begin and end each day with a kiss. Say, "Hello." Say, "Good-bye." Follow the advice of a great song from the 60s and "Seal It With A Kiss."

Y: Create a loving relationship with yourself. Live your life. As much as possible, say, "Yes!" to life.

Z: Live and love from within the mind-free zone from Chapter 2.

A-Z Add Your Own Words: I am not going to recreate *Webster's Dictionary* and highlight every word in the English language. So if you feel there are any words I missed and failed to mention, please feel free to add them to their appropriate letter and explain why you feel each word is an important ingredient in every successful relationship. (If you are lucky enough to have the workbook, there is room for this. Or you can add a list to your Noteworthy Notes file.)

In an effort to foreshadow this chapter's final section, I suggest you re-read the ABCs as much as possible, and apply all the words to *A GLOBAL WE!*

Time-Transitions

This fourth category is the one most often overlooked or fully forgotten. If you truly wish to organize and master your new and improved holistic-self, then it is imperative you intentionally focus and pay attention to it. This is because the category of time-transitions is the foundation of the four-file system.

Think of the first three categories of self, occupations, and relationships as the bed, desk, and closet in my big brother's room. When you walk on the floor, the room's foundation, you can *physically* move your body from one place to another. In parallel, when you use your unique methods of time-transitions, the four-file system's foundation, you can *mentally* move your focus and attention from one category to another.

And only when you focus and pay attention to the big picture, and solidly set your life in a completely organized, SORTed four-file system, will you rightly realize how your self, occupations, and relationships are all holistically healthier and easier to manage. When you incorporate the last foundational category of Time-Transitions, you will also realize how your life is dramatically less stressful. With these two key realizations set, it stands to reason, your life will be profoundly more productive and accordingly, abundantly more fantastically fun!

An additional analogy for this concept, is a full concert orchestra. When performing a piece of music, each instrument can play an independent, un-social, solo part, or all the instruments can play together in a social, ensemble group. When all the instruments are performing on the same stage, a foundational floor, it is how the composer and the conductor transitions, and uses different tempos, volumes, and solo versus ensemble play, which artfully makes the music unique.

Again, in parallel, when it comes to organizing and managing your new and improved, holistic self, you write the song of *Your Life*. In short, *you completely compose yourself!*

Exercise 13 - Compose Yourself: Set Your Present-Day Life-Speeds and Create Your Character's Concerto!

You can use the pages in your workbook to write your answers, or use your own paper.

Step 1: Set your pulse pace. This is your internal tempo.

On a scale of 1 to 10 with your thoughts and emotions, are you a little slow (1), or are you quick as a whip (10)? Does this position work for you? Yes or No?

If No, write five things to work on, which you believe will help you improve your score.

Step 2: Set your rhythm of life. This is your external tempo.

On a scale of 1 to 10 on the road of life, are you a little slow (1) or are you living in the fast lane (10)? Does this position work for you? Yes or No?

If No, write five things to work on, which you believe will help you improve your score.

Do your best to think of some self-help ideas that may or may not be listed in this book. If you need help, simply ask a trusted teacher.

Step 3: If you are satisfied, and you believe your present positions do work for you, then WOW! That's wonderful!

If not, immediately implement your ten new self-help ideas and willingly work on composing yourself.

Lonely vs. Alone

First, look at the big picture and find your place in it. Realize there are approximately 8.2 billion people on this planet. For all you natural nature lovers out there, the population of living things on this planet is incalculable! So if you think of Earth as your holistic home, then you will never truly feel alone ever again. Second, if this concept is not quite crystal clear for you yet, then see the movie *Contact*. In it, the main character, played by Jodie Foster, talks about the size of the whole universe. She says, "If it's just us, then it's an awful big waste of space." This is a classic Search for Extraterrestrial Intelligence (SETI) Carl Sagan quote. And in the science world, it is a fairly common philosophical line of reasoning. In short, odds are we are not alone in the universe.

Here's the benefit to *knowing* you are not alone. When you find yourself *feeling lonely*, simply follow the advice of the old AT&T phone commercials. First, determine where you are in relation to everyone else. Second, by whatever means necessary, do as the slogan says, "Reach out and touch someone." Or you can consciously choose to change your nasty, negative, lonely feelings, into positive, peaceful, *only alivingly alone* feelings. Subsequently, you can use these new feelings as fuel for productive solo time. And, when you have done this enough times, you will know you have successfully learned Life Lesson 2: Pain vs. Suffering from Chapter 3. You will know, as M. Kathleen Casey has been quoted saying, "Pain is inevitable. Suffering is optional." And you will also know, you most definitely do have a choice! When you feel lonely, don't let the feeling fester!

Lifetime Role Models: MAGIC and Sail the Seven Cs!

"Sir" Charles Barkley is listed in *The Top 50 Greatest NBA Players of All Time*. He has always been good for a tell-it-like-it-is sports sound bite or a cool, colorful commentary. In one of the most famous sports commercials of all time, Sir Charles made the claim, "I am not a role model." This controversial comment sent waves of confusion throughout all the sports fans who ultimately asked, "Then who are our role models?"

My answers for them, and my advice to you, are as follows: First, create MAGIC. Second, Sail the Seven Cs. MAGIC is an acronym for Make A Good Intelligent Choice. The Seven Cs are used to form the following sentence and positive piece of advice: Collect Cool Companions and Consciously Choose them with Clear Criteria. With this in mind, do the following exercise:

Exercise 14 - Discover Who's Been Your Past-to-Present LRMs (Lifetime Role Models) and Determine Your Clear Criteria to be a Future LRM

Step 1: Create a Non-Fictional People Dinner Party Guests List.

The people can be living or dead.

Step 2: Create a Fictional Characters Dinner Party Guests List.

The characters can be anyone or anything.

Step 3: For each guest on each list, create a Top Ten Admirable Character Traits List.

Remember: *It is your dinner party!*

Step 4: Compile your Admirable Character Traits Lists and this will become your clear criteria. Refer back to these lists to choose future LRMs.

Set Your (Mind's) Set: It Takes All Kinds to Make a World!

When you have finally finished the lifetime role models exercise, you are more than halfway home to achieving the goals of this last section. First, develop a whole world, whole humanity, global point of view. Second, see how your LRMs are all connected in a Constellation of Characters. Third, know a fundamental truth: you create your own reality and fact and fiction, it takes all kinds to make a world!

Developing a whole-world, whole-humanity, global overview, occurs when you purposely set your mind-set. Before saying you are an "American" or an "Any-other-an," consider yourself to be, first and foremost, an "Earthling." Or if you emphatically insist on using the "an" ending, then call yourself a "Planetarian." And instead of "Mankind" use "Humankind." Consciously transpose your titles and terms. Make these small, subtle, semantic changes. Doing this will literally make a world of difference. For I honestly do believe someday soon, this mindset-revolution, will in fact *dramatically* change the world.

And the next step is to visualize how your lifetime role models and the whole planetary population, are in fact clearly connected. In short, embrace the theory of Six Degrees of Separation. This states how six steps, or degrees, directly connect each person to every other person on the planet. (See the 1993 movie starring Stockard Channing, Donald Sutherland, and a very young Will Smith. Also play the Hollywood networking game, Six Degrees of Kevin Bacon.) To creatively depict this paradigm, do the following exercise:

Exercise 15 - Lifetime Role Models: Draw Your Constellations of Characters

Step 1: Review your lifetime role model lists.

Step 2: Think of these people and characters as the "stars of your life."

Step 3: As if you are putting together a family tree or creating a star chart, draw a picture which shows how you are all connected to each other. On the branches, or next to each star, write the criteria information you will need to show how each person or character connects to you and fits into your life's big picture.

Step 4: With all the artistic ability you can muster, and as if you were your past's youthful, inner child, or six-year-old self, embellish your drawing with multi-colors, glow-in-the-dark star stickers, or 3D texture. Use items such as yarn, pom-poms, glitter glue, and/or whatever else your little art-heart desires.

Step 5: Hang your Constellation of Characters on a Wall of Fame.

Step 6: Step back and take a good, long look at your Constellation of Characters, life's big picture. See how it's filled with both non-fictional, factual people, and fictionally created characters. Remember how every day you are making conscious or unconscious choices to keep these people and characters in your life. See how these LRMs helped you develop your overview of the whole world and appreciate how they intuitively and/or intrinsically inspired you to create your own reality.

Step 7: Use this picture to achieve the last goal of this section. *Look at it and know the fundamental truth: you create your own reality and it takes all kinds to make a world!*

[Use the space below to do your first rough draft, basic sketchings and designs etc.]

And that is the end of this section. After a quick post view, we can continue our sweet sailings and begin Chapter 5: The Heart of Your Art!

Post View

In the theater world, you have Set the Stage! Congratulations! Your ship has finally arrived at its pre-performance port. It is the perfect time to tie up all loose lines and take stock of what you have got. For a moment, look back with self-admiration.

You have completed the following four sections:

- SORT Your Life into a Four-File System
- Lonely vs. Alone
- Lifetime Role Models: MAGIC and Sail the Seven Cs
- Set Your (Mind's) Set: It Takes All Kinds to Make a World!

You have completed the following five exercises:

- Daily-Debriefing: A Present Detoxification Process
- Plot A Week's Worth of Spending: Create a Color-Coded Time Occupations Bar Graph
- Compose Yourself: Set Your Present-Day Life-Speeds and Create Your Character's Concerto!
- Lifetime Role Models: Discover Who's Been Your Past-To-Present LRMs and Determine Your Clear Criteria for future LRMs
- Lifetime Role Models: Draw Your Constellations of Characters

Lastly, you have completed two more of The 16 Secrets of Success.

10. Organize your life. Find a system that works for you.

 You have created a user-friendly, SORTed Four-File System. Your social versus un-social self is set. Your occupations, or how you spend your time, is set. Your ABCs of a successful relationship is set. And your time-transitions, foundational floor is set. In short, you have efficiently SORTed and organized your life!

11. Create a clear picture of the world. See how it is all connected.

 You have created a tangible, visual aide, artistic representation of your Constellation of Characters. You see your life's big picture posted on your Wall of Fame, and you know your place in it. Your view of the world is clear. You see how you and all your lifetime role models are connected. In short, you have sufficiently Set the Stage!

You have done all these things successfully. *YOU GO! YOU ARE THE CHARACTER!* Okay. Now turn the page. Our journey continues in Chapter 5: The Heart of Your Art!

CHAPTER 5:
THE HEART OF YOUR ART!

Preview

All right! Action! Scene 5! One of the lesser-known quotes from Shakespeare's *Hamlet* is said by Queen Gertrude to the long-winded Polonius. She urges him to get to the point by saying, "More matter less art." In the past four chapters, you have discovered the real matter of your character. You are crystal clear about your presentized self. You are a human doing who now knows how to focus and pay attention, easily ask for help, and honorably earn it. You holistically see the scene and you have successfully set the stage. The purpose of this chapter is to bring all these concepts together. This way you will be greater than the sum of all your parts. So now, energetically empower yourself to enthusiastically establish The Heart of Your Art!

The first section is Attitude and Passion: Eliminate Forecasting FEAR (False Expectations Apparent Realities)! Do What FUELs (Full-Filling Unconditionally Enthusiastically Love) You! Here you will adjust your attitude and empower yourself with passion. You will create one side of your character teeter-totter. Do you remember this playground fixture that had two people sitting on a board on a fulcrum, across from each other, and using their legs to push themselves up and down, alternately? It is a great physical description of what it is like to manage FEAR. You will learn the real meaning of FEAR, and you will overcome your initial and instinctive feelings of FEAR. Thus, you will conquer any control it has over you. And finally, you will productively use your newly acquired surplus time and energy to do what FUELs you.

The second section is Be Perceptive from Your Perspective! Be Persistent to Your Purpose! Here you will establish the other side of your character teeter-totter and you will initiate a balance between the two sides. You will learn how to develop a real-life stage presence. You will read about Thomas Edison, a.k.a. Mr. Results. Using Edison as the ultimate example, you will see how if necessity is the mother of invention, then persistence is the father of success. You will reward yourself for how far you have come and you will infuse yourself with a renewed sense of energized enthusiasm and courageous confidence. You will refocus on your real reason for reading this book and on your overall purpose in life. This recharging of your bio-batteries will carry you through the book's last two chapters, down the home stretch, and all the way through to the FANTASTIC-ly fabulous, final finish line.

The third section is Content and Comfortable vs. Happy and Hungry! Here you will determine which side of Billy Joel's "River of Dreams" you are on. You will know if you are stuck on the shore or floating down the river. (Another great message song, which parallels this paradigm, is Garth Brooks "Standing Outside the Fire.") And once you have made this reality realization, you will ultimately make a completely life-changing conscious choice, and you will make a dramatic decision. As Andy Dufresne (Tim Robbins) says to his friend Ellis Boyd "Red" Redding (Morgan Freeman) in *The Shawshank Redemption*, it will be, "time to get busy living or get busy dying." By the end of the chapter, you will have answered the questions, "What is your life attitude?" and, "What are you going to 'get busy' doing?" *Remember, it is your one and only life! It is your choice! Make it a great one!*

Attitude and Passion: Eliminate Forecasting FEAR!
Do What FUELs You!

When you are in a scene, whether it is theatrical or real, *nothing influences the result more, than your attitude.* It is one side of your character's teeter-totter and it is your heart's and mind's ultimate internal processor. In parallel, Zig Ziglar said, "Your attitude, not your aptitude, will determine your altitude." Or, you can be an extreme external top talent, but if you do not have an overtly optimistic, "I believe in me." attitude, to balance your talent, then you will never actually achieve any high level of supreme success.

I have a female friend (the same one from A Perfect You and Are you attractive?) who in our first meeting, her mother asked me one of the greatest character defining questions I have ever heard. She asked, "Putting all religious connotations aside, is the universe friendly?"

Wow! I thought for a second. Then I said, "Yes. I believe it is."

I will never forget her response. She said to her delightful daughter, "Yep. He's a keeper." I guess she figured once she knew where I stood in relation to the universe, I would be equally positive and optimistic with her daughter. Well apparently, *after forty years,* she was completely right to have such high hopes and faith in our friendship.

Exercise 16 - Attitude: Is the Universe Friendly?

Step 1: Ask yourself this quintessential question and write your best attitude answer: Is the universe friendly?

Step 2: Explain the reasons for your answer.

Step 3: Write how this attitude is expressed in your everyday life.

Step 4: If you think the universe is unfriendly, brainstorm ideas how you can positively adjust your attitude. If you already think the universe is friendly, then I say, "Outstanding!"

Step 5: Put your, "unfriendly to friendly" ideas into practice and record your results in the workbook. Or record your examples/evidence of the universe's friendliness.

Tony Robbins said, "Motivation is like a warm bath. It is nice while it lasts, but eventually you need to get out of the tub. When you find activities you are passionate about, that is when you will have positive, productive energy to last a lifetime." I have never heard a better explanation of the difference between the two energies of momentary motivation and permanent passion. With this said, my questions are, "What stops us from venturing out, finding, and doing any of these self-empowering activities," and, "Who is Shakespeare's 'smiling, vile villain,' who steals from us our possible FANTASTIC future?" I am here to tell you, that foul philistine, is FEAR!

Franklin D. Roosevelt said, "The only thing we have to fear is fear itself." Yes. Especially when you learn the real meaning of the word FEAR. It means False Expectations Apparent Realities. This acronym definition tells us how the mere projection of our imagination can be much more debilitating and dangerous to our intellectual psyche than any actual reality could ever be. We know this to be true, whenever we watch any sci-fi, suspense, horror, alien, or monster movie. What we see with our mind's eye is always a million times more frightening than any special effect movie magic image. And the same can be said about the mind's ear. If you want a seemingly scary movie to be a lot less startling, simply turn off the sound. When the screams of terror and the bloodcurdling, creepy, menacing music is suddenly missing, the silent images, sometimes surprisingly so, no longer have any real emotional effect on us.

Now I know you have questions: "How does this all apply to everyday real life FEAR?" "When I am feeling nervous, worried, anxious, and/or I am simply scared out of my mind, what should I do?" "How can I conquer my FEAR?" *The answer is you control your FEAR.* Do not let your FEAR control you. Recognize FEAR is only in your mind. Realize you can consciously choose a course of courage and matter over mind. Transcend and treat your FEAR as if it parallels pain. Remember the life lesson you learned in Chapter 3: See the Scene!

Silently say, "FEAR is synonymous with pain. FEAR is inevitable. Staying stuck and paralyzed in the grip of FEAR is optional." And with this conscious choice I choose wisely. For I know I cannot completely eliminate my initial, *instinctive* feelings of FEAR. But I can eradicate, and totally do away with, woefully worrying and wasting my time and energy on forecasting FEAR into my real-ly unknown and truly unforeseeable future. So instead of impractically panicking due to a made-up proposed possibility of calamity or chaos, I know I can consciously choose to apply a little calm courage, take immediate action, and create the circumstances I real-ly do desire. And I know I can do this with complete confidence. I can, I will, and I do, boldly move fantastically forward. This is my life! I have total control over all my FEARs! My advice, make these self-speak statements your masterful mind's mantra. Write them out on note cards and carry them with you—*always*.

And after you have practiced doing this a few times, you will soon realize just how much FEAR-free surplus time and energy you now have available to you. And you will also realize how you can ultimately use this time and energy for much more productive purposes. And the greatest productive purpose of all is to channel your passion toward finding and doing all the activities which FUEL you! This means performing all the activities you find Full-Filling and you Unconditionally and Enthusiastically Love doing!

And now, here is a declaration of truth and the big payoff for this section: There is nothing on Earth, more powerful than a young-at-heart, confident and courageous character, who can consciously adjust their attitude, who can empower themselves with positive productive passion, who can eliminate forecasting FEAR, and who can find and do all the amazing activities which FUEL their lives! And, if you believe your character is an unquestionably qualified member of this real life special-forces group, then you have astoundingly achieved the greatest of goals, and you have amazingly arrived at an enormously impressive milestone marker, on the course of your character's evolutionary and joyful journey!

Question: What is the potential power of this kind of Special Forces group?

Answer: "You should never doubt that a small group of thoughtful, committed citizens can change the world; indeed, it is the only thing that ever has." ~ Margaret Mead

Be Perceptive from Your Perspective! Be Persistent to Your Purpose!

The last section describes how attitude is the most influential factor in all interpersonal interactions. It illustrates how attitude is the power pump for your heart's and mind's *internal* processor. On the other side of your character teeter-totter are your perceptions. With these *external* sensors, you gather all the available bits of data and diligently download them into your central computer—a.k.a. your brain.

If you want your character teeter-totter—your life—to be balanced, your attitude and your perceptions must work together. For example, if you want your attitude's outlook to be, "rosy," your eyes must, "view the world through rose-colored glasses." The same rule applies for all other senses. Just as in Chapter 3 when you used all specialized sights to, "see with better eyes," when you are balanced, you are also able to hear, smell, taste, and touch with better ears, nose, mouth, and body. Subsequently, your ability to control your life dramatically increases and your character's self-empowerment and life evolution positively progresses.

If you want a creative visualization to use in tandem with this concept, then picture yourself perfectly balanced and confidently standing on the fulcrum of your life's character teeter-totter. This is your perfect point of view—life's perspective. And if you are always able to consciously visualize yourself experiencing the world from this position of supreme confidence, then, as the title character in "The Adventures of Buckaroo Banzai Across the 8th Dimension" says, "No matter where you go, there you are." And when you are able to acquire this extremely enlightened, externally visible energy, your holistic character will go way beyond just having the basic character traits of charm or charisma. When you enter a room, everybody will take notice. You will have an unmistakable, power-full-ly magnetic, amazing aura of real life, spectacular stage presence.

For the next step, the question becomes, "Once I have acquired this stage presence, presentized energy, character trait, how do I productively use it to help me build my character for the future?" Well, successful people from all walks of life have answered this question with catch phrases such as daily dedication, tough tenacity, or consistent commitment. They all mean the same thing: we are talking about positive persistence.

The ultimate example of someone who extremely excelled in his daily display of this particular character trait was Thomas A. Edison. Edison famously described this tenacity in several ways: One, "Many of life's failures are people who did not realize how close they were to success when they quit and gave up." Two, "Opportunity is missed by most people because it is dressed in overalls and looks like work." And three, "There is no substitute for hard work." In short, positive persistence is paramount.

There is a famous anecdote behind the creative course of events, which led to the invention of the incandescent light bulb. The story goes, Edison tried over 10,000 experiments before he finally found the right kind of filament material which would burn the brightest and last the longest. During the process, a reporter asked Edison if it was frustrating not getting any results, after so many attempts. Edison responded, "Results! Why man! I've gotten lots of results! I've found several thousand things that won't work!"

Finally, if you approach all your life ambitions with this same optimistic attitude, positive perspective, and high degree of discipline, dedication, and passionate, purposeful persistence, then I can practically guarantee you will achieve a long-lasting level of success, which will burn brighter than any bulb Edison ever built.

Note: You determine your definition of success. We will explore this concept in greater detail in Chapter 6: The Curtain Call!

Content and Comfortable vs. Happy and Hungry!

The origin of this concept occurred when I realized not one, "Once upon a time ..." story ever ended with the phrase, "... and they all lived comfortably ever after," or "... and they were both content for the rest of their lives." No. In the end, every story promises the characters are going to be, "happy." Admittedly as an interested reader or listener, this news was nice to hear, but in my mind, it forever fell short of satisfaction. I always wanted to know what happens after the last happily ever after line? *Exactly how* do they live their happily ever after, long life?

My theory is as follows: happiness is a very unstable state. I say this because when a character does achieve this natural high psychological summit, I think it is impossible to sustain it indefinitely. For as soon as time is added to the mix, happiness gets redefined and subsequently subsides, until it becomes basic contentment, or just a simple state of *being* comfortable. Not to mention that our goals can shift and change with time and things that once seemed unattainable become commonplace and everyday doable. In a growth mindset we are always upleveling.

So how should you deal with this situation? When you find yourself alive-ly living in a state of happiness, just listen to the old Bobby McFerrin song and, "Don't Worry. Be Happy." Then when your happiness eventually settles into its stagnant state, or comfort zone, that is the time to become proactive and reestablish your new fact foundation. Use this stable stance platform to leap up and forward, onto your next life's high point. In short, you wonderfully arrive at your next high, happy home.

69

Note: A point needs to be made. This "leap up" is not a long-shot, bad odds gamble. That would be a loser's leap. Because when you take those kinds of risks, the house always wins. In this case, you are arriving at a new home. When you reach this special place, your new home base, you end up scoring high points in your game of life. This is the truly successful, winner's way to play.

What is the driving force behind these leaps of faith? It is the feeling of being hopeful and hungry. Lee Ann Womack reminds us in her song "I Hope You Dance" to continue to be hungry, but always get your fill. This is a prime description of the pinnacle emotional state, which I believe is literally vital for all human doings. Yes. I feel it is that important! There are always new ways to view the world and to find the happiness we seek.

Throughout history, humankind has shown how it needs something to strive toward, to thrive and grow. The best example of this is powered flight and the space race. The time interval from December 17th, 1903, when the Wright brothers took their first flight, to July 20th, 1969, when Neil Armstrong climbed out of Apollo 11 and took his first step on the moon, *was only sixty-six years!* By geological standards, that's barely a blink in time. So much progress in such a short period of time is simply astronomical! Please pardon the space pun.

So subsequently, if you listen to the following three pieces of advice, your life can be transformed into a joyful journey on a summit-less spiral. You will flow upwards from one state of hungry to the next state of happy. As you continue to travel up, you will MAGIC-ally manifest extreme examples of personal growth, and you will successfully accomplish all your golden goals.

Three Pieces of Advice: (These provide my recipe for a happy and hungry life.)

1. Be hungry! Review everything you have learned from this book. Visualize your next, "meal." Passionately pounce on it. Eat your fill. Then…

2. Be happy! Feel the feeling all the way through to your own holistic full-fill-ment. Then …

3. Give yourself time and repeat the process as often as possible!

Now here you are finishing the final turn and dashing down the home stretch. You have traversed through five chapters of my TaylorED Time: How to Dramatically Build Your Character & Live the Life FANTASTIC! After a quick post view, you can move on to Chapter 6: The Curtain Call!

Post View

Welcome home. You have arrived at the heart of your art. This is where you have presently discovered what is in all your gifts. You now know the answer to the question, "What is the matter of your heart?" In short, *you now know the content of your character.*

So for a moment, look back again with self-admiration.

You have completed the following three sections:

- Attitude and Passion: Eliminate Forecasting FEARs and Do What FUELs You!
- Be Perceptive from Your Perspective and Be Persistent to Your Purpose!
- Content and Comfortable vs. Happy and Hungry!

You have completed the following one exercise:

- Attitude: Is the Universe Friendly?

You have completed two more of The 16 Secrets of Success.

12. Adjust your attitude. Empower your passion. Eliminate forecasting FEARs (False Expectations Apparent Realities)! Do what FUELs (Full-filling Unconditionally Enthusiastically Love) You!

    You did these in the first section.

13. Be perceptive from your perspective! Be persistent to your purpose! Never settle for *only* content and comfortable. *Also,* always strive for holistically happy and hungry! *Never give up! … Don't quit! … EVER!*

    You did these in the second and third sections.

Clearly these two secrets of success are not exactly secrets. For if you look at any person who, by reasonable standards, is commonly thought of as being successful, then I will bet that person already knows about all these concepts, in one form or another. As Tom Hanks, a very successful human doing, once said as the title character in the movie Forest Gump, "That is all I have to say about that." You have done all these things successfully! *YOU GO! YOU ARE THE CHARACTER!* Okay. Now turn the page. Our journey continues in Chapter 6: The Curtain Call!

CHAPTER 6:
THE CURTAIN CALL!

Preview

All right! Action! Scene 6! This chapter's title serves a double meaning and the content has a dual purpose. In the theater world, the curtain call takes place at two different times during the production. The first is the specific time the ensemble, cast, and crew are scheduled to arrive at the theater. The second comes at the end of each show, when all the bows and curtsies are taken, when all the music conductors and VIPs are acknowledged, and (hopefully) when the whole audience applauds and shows their appreciation for all the hard work done on their behalf.

The first type of curtain call is usually seen symbolically as the end of the rehearsal process. For you, as we near the end of our journey, I will simply list several character conclusions. The second type of curtain call is both an ending and a beginning. The production day is over. The next new adventure begins tomorrow. Here is where *our* journey ends and *your* journey begins. This is where you do your own character continuations, supported by the workbook.

In this section there will be three special sub-sections.

They are as follows:

1. Get GIGSS (Gather In Group Support Systems)

   Note To All Teenagers and College/University Students: Exercise 17 will show you how to do a Character Clique Switch Week. Follow the steps, learn a few very valuable life lessons, and most importantly, have fun.

2. Celebrate Family and Friends!

3. Create Unity and Community!

Character Conclusions

1) Be your own character-ship's captain. We talked about this concept way back in Chapter 1: Character Crystallization! Whenever you engage in any kind of production process for constructing and creating your own character-ship, *make sure you are clearly its captain!* In the next section, read and sign a Character Commitment Contract. This way you will make a formal commitment to a lifetime of personal growth and you will put it in writing.

2) Be on a mission. Again, in Chapter 1 we talked about how you need to Find True (For You) North. Now you are on the right track for reaching your goals and getting what you want. See your life as a mission of global importance. In the next section, write your own *My Mission Statement, My Purpose in Life Paragraph*, and *My Definition of Success Story*. And as you write these inspired items, repeat this mantra, "I will dream big! I will manifest best!"

3) Create, plan, and write your own funeral, epitaph, and eulogy. This is a classic, creative visualization, post-success, life affirming activity. And it is also a wonderful way to easily express a unique perspective on your life. Remember, you will not be there to witness or enjoy your event, and yet it should still reflect how you wish your life to be remembered. This is also a great way to forge and facilitate a living legacy and to positively preview your own FANTASTIC future.

4) Take total responsibility for your life. Stan Lee, the creator of Spider-man, said, "With great power comes great responsibility." I was recently reminded of this quintessential quote, and was instantly inspired to apply it to my own life. And I put a special spin on it. My thoughts are as follows: If you choose to travel on a path of self-empowerment, and if you strive to acquire super-self-powers, then successfully DOING all your new and improved actions will be your response-abilities.

In short, take total responsibility for your life, achieve greatness through a positive, productive process of self-empowerment, and live your life doing all your response-abilities. (And remember, this was one of the most important, highlighted R words, listed in The ABCs of a Successful Relationship.)

5) Take the path less traveled. In Robert Frost's poem "The Road Less Traveled," he wrote, "… I took the path less traveled by, and that has made all the difference." My advice follows these same lines. I say, when you choose the path of your life, do not be ordinary. Do not be an unconscious conformist to society. Do not just live your life blindly re-acting. Instead, endeavor to be EXTRAORDINARY! Make it your life's ambition to FEARlessly forge your own positive, productive path, in the forest of your future.

6) True and FANTASTIC freedom for all, only exists in a state of total tolerance. (This is a big picture concept, so please read these next two paragraphs carefully.) Every human being, and human doing, on this planet, is a holistically special singularity. This means *everyone creates his or her own character* by gathering information with his or her own particular perception of external reality, and interpreting that information with his or her own individual internal, personality processors. *This also means, for all humans to be truly and FANTASTIC-ally free, all humans must totally tolerate all manifestations of all humans—EVERYWHERE!*

In the movie *The American President,* Michael Douglas, playing President Andrew Shepherd, says, "Let's see you acknowledge a man whose words make your blood boil, who is standing center stage and advocating at the top of his lungs that which you would spend a lifetime opposing at the top of yours." For me, this quote represents total tolerance of diversity. And I believe it is a major, moral imperative, you support and validate these foundational values. *And when you do create your own reality, you must also respect other people's right to do the same for their own reality.* And on top of that, when a system of government, and the laws of the land, are specifically designed to support and protect these rights, *I believe that is a definitive example of what it real-ly means to live in a totally true and solid state of FANTASTIC FREEDOM FOR ALL!*

7) Lasagna. On occasion I am asked, "Of all your lifetime role models, whose opinion do you value most?" By far, the penultimate prize goes to my parents. Throughout my whole life, they have always been there for me, with steadfast supper support, timely tough love, and poignantly placed, tailored Taylor-ings. And the absolute best, anecdotal example of one of these parental points, is simply known in my family as— and here it is in all its grotesque gastric glory—The Lasagna Story.

When I was a pre-teen, I had the extreme misfortune of having a bad bout with serious stomach flu. Now it needs to be mentioned, both my parents are in the medical profession. So suffice it to say, they knew what to do and appropriately put me on a clear liquid, soft food diet. I was barely able to keep that down. Then after I had been home from school for almost a week, I reached my breaking point. I was tired, frustrated, and I decided I did not want to be sick anymore. So I told my parents, "I don't care what it is, I am going to eat real food for supper." They calmly gave me their opinions.

My mother said, "I don't think it's such a good idea, but okay, if you insist." I guess she saw I was in my steadfast, stubborn mode.

My father started with his classic opening question, "Do you want my opinion?" I said, "What!" (Forever after I have learned the only real answer to this question is, "Yes." But, what can I say? Back then I was young and foolish, and now, well that's another book.) Anyway, Dad pushed through my pre-teen defiance and said, "We are having lasagna. You should not eat it because you will not keep it down, and you will get violently ill."

I repeated my mantra, "I don't care!"

So, Dad said his classic closing line, "Okay. I have spoken."

Well, without going into the completely colorful, disgusting details, Dad was right. And after about forty-five minutes of praying to the porcelain God, I came out of the bathroom white as a sheet. My parents were waiting for me. First, they asked, "Are you okay?"

I said, "Yes."

Then my dad said, "Good. Now listen carefully. For the rest of your life, when your mother and I give you our opinions, and we don't think you are going to take them, and we feel your safety and/or your personal well-being are in impending danger, then we are going to simply say to you, 'Lasagna.' Then, hopefully, you will remember this gratuitously grotesque, minor moment, you will reconsider your position, and you will trustingly take our opinions on faith." To this day, The Lasagna Card has been a priceless, parental tool.

I tell you this story to colorfully illustrate one of the countless reasons why I value my parents' opinion over all others, and why I designate them as my primary LRMs. If you remember in Chapter 4: Set the Stage!, you consciously choose your lifetime role models using self-determined clear criteria. Make sure you continue this practice. Whenever an opinion or any advice is given, always assess its value by first considering the source of who said it. Never unconsciously or cavalierly relinquish control over your choices. *Always remember it is your life! You create your own reality and you determine your own destiny!*

Character Continuations

1) Create a Character Commitment Contract. I am including a copy of my fill-in-the-blank form. I use this in my own public speaking presentations. You are welcome to use it as a tried-and-true template to create your own version.

   Directions: Make a formal commitment to lifelong learning and personal growth and put it in writing. Include the date. Print your name. Sign your name. And—this last ingredient is incredibly important—choose two to four of your LRMs and have them perform a sign of support. Ask them to sign their names and be a witness to you making and signing your Character Commitment Contract. Then cut it out and post it in a prominent place. (You can also buy Contracts of Commitment and Certificates of Success on my website: TaylorEDTime.com)

Character Commitment Contract

I, _____, do solemnly swear and sign, I am making a conscious and complete commitment, to positively producing my character's creation.

I will also continue the process far beyond the completion of reading and writing in this book and its companion workbook. In all my worldly travels, I will be the captain of my character ship! And if, as Shakespeare said, "All the world's a stage," then in the play of my life, I will always be the LEAD-ER!

Your signature:_____   Date _____/_____/_____

Sign of support:_____   Date _____/_____/_____

Sign of support:_____   Date _____/_____/_____

Sign of support:_____   Date _____/_____/_____

Sign of support:_____   Date _____/_____/_____

---

2) Create a My Mission Statement and My Purpose in Life Paragraph. A mission is a spiritual, lifelong process which requires definitive action and commitment. You are here on Earth to co-create your destiny and to accomplish the golden goal of fulfilling your life's purpose. As an example, the following is My Mission Statement and My Purpose in Life Paragraph.

My Mission Statement and My Purpose in Life Paragraph

I believe I was born to supply something great to human history and to live abundantly alive! So I dramatically devote myself to tenaciously teaching as many people as possible to passionately, persistently, and productively produce the highest and healthiest vision and version of themselves. The extremely essential and extraordinary role which I willingly want to purposefully play is to facilitate as many lifelong learning love-a-lots to consciously create their coolest character and to BEAUTIFULly balance their best self with a harmoniously helpful, pleasantly peaceful, and gloriously gorgeous, global community. My meaning and my major reason for doing what I do is for me to tenaciously teach humanity's leaders of tomorrow to MAGIC-ally manifest the present gift of a real reality where the whole human race can confidently forecast a holistically healthy and a fabulously FANTASTIC, FEAR-free future. And my final fact is no one can live my life exactly the way I do. Consequently I have developed certain specific talents and skills and I believe being holistically myself is inherently a unique talent and skill unto itself. So whenever I experience a love of something or someone, I know this is a unique gift. I also know it is the graciously giving of this gift, in service of others, which defines my main mission in life. My true happiness is only achieved when I am absolutely aligned with this positive paradigm. *IN CONCLUSION, I BELIEVE MY LIFETIME'S USE OF MY UNIQUE GIFTS IS THE REAL REASON I CREATIVELY CAME TO BE ALIVE TO DO WHAT I DO, IN AND WITH MY HOLISTICALLY FANTASTIC LIFE!*

ALIVINGLY42! A+ ☺ *Andrew S. Taylor*

Now, write your own My Mission Statement and My Purpose in Life Paragraph. Use the spaces/lines on the next page.

My Mission Statement and My Purpose in Life Paragraph

_____

_____

_____

_____

_____

_____

_____

_____

_____

_____

_____

_____

_____

_____

_____

_____

_____

_____

_____

_____

_____

If you need more space, use the workbook pages.

3) Write a My Definition of Success Story. While I was doing the research for this book, I discovered several definitions of what it means to be a success. I compiled them into a list of observations. I hope this will be a valuable, thought-provoking tool. I hope it will help you write your own Definition of Success Story. *(And always remember, success is a Lifetime Achievement Award! ... Never give up! ... Don't quit! ... EVER!)*

Success: A List of Observations

1. Success is the end of our striving and the beginning of our thriving.

2. Success is the manifesting of our desires, the reaching of our goals, and the achieving of our dreams.

3. Success is a result, and there are as many recipes for success as there are people. (If you enthusiastically enjoy the journey, it is a big-time bonus!)

4. Success can be personally private and/or particularly public.

5. The definition of success can change in a heartbeat or slowly over time.

6. Young people usually define success using materialistic terms: physical items, a.k.a. fame and fortune, and/or living the lotto-life, which provides the finances for a plethora of possibilities for purchasing power.

7. Older, more experienced people, usually define success using more intangible terms: intellectual, emotional, and spiritual standards, a.k.a. priceless and true treasures.

8. And as we achieve our milestone markers of success, new ones will *always* appear on the horizon. Continuing to sail towards these golden goals is a prime example of what it means to stay hungry.

Another helpful tool is using the following quote as a success-full, lifetime checklist.

"That person is a success ...

... who has lived well, laughed often, and loved much.

... who has gained the respect of intelligent people, and the love of children.

... who has filled their niche and accomplished their task.

... who leaves the world better than they found it.

... who looked for the best in others and gave the best they had to give."

~ Robert Louis Stevenson

Now use these two tools as guides to help write your own My Definition of Success Story.

My Definition of Success Story

_____

_____

_____

_____

_____

_____

_____

_____

_____

_____

_____

_____

_____

_____

_____

_____

_____

_____

If you need more space, use the workbook pages.

4) Create, plan, and write your own Funeral, Epitaph, and Eulogy. At first glance this may seem like a morbidly macabre and pessimistic assignment. But I am hoping in the end you will see it as the exact opposite. I hope when you are finished you will see it as an all-encompassing, learn-how-to-leave-your-legacy, overtly-optimistic, life-affirming assignment.

Here is a helpful hint. Maintain the following mini-mantra in your mind: I will dream big! I will manifest best! With this internal focus, your mind's eye simply will not be able to foresee any kind of event or ceremony, which usually marks the end of an all too short, unsatisfactory, and unfulfilled life. On the contrary, with this creative visualization mindset, you will clearly be able to see countless family and friends expressing thoughts and feelings such as, "He/She did so much in their life. I am amazed they were able to find all the time and energy they needed to do it so successfully!" And/Or, "He/She was so healthy and happy for such a long life. That is really rare these days!" And/Or, "Wow! They made such a difference in the lives of so many and were so professionally successful and so personally loved! I am sure they will be remembered fondly for several generations to come!"

Okay. Now create, plan, and write your own My Funeral, Epitaph, and Eulogy. And know that this exercise is much more than mere make-believe. *It is masterfully manifesting and MAGIC-ally making it all happily happen!* For when you create powerful tools to creatively visualize your future, it helps others know you better, and it also helps make your foreseen future, finally and fruitfully come to fruition. And make sure your top two or four lifetime role models officially make signs of support and add vital validation dates at the bottom.

My Funeral, Epitaph, and Eulogy

_____

_____

_____

_____

_____

_____

_____

_____

_____

_____

_____

_____

_____

_____

_____

_____

_____

_____

_____

_____

Your signature:_____   Date _____/_____/_____

Sign of support:_____   Date _____/_____/_____

Sign of support:_____   Date _____/_____/_____

Sign of support:_____   Date _____/_____/_____

Sign of support:_____   Date _____/_____/_____

If you need more space, use the workbook pages.

5) Nothing is written in stone … not yet. Okay. You have planned your funeral. You have written your epitaph and eulogy. And you have carved your final dates and your last words in your headstone. No. Wait a minute. Back up. Go back to that last one. Nothing is written in stone … not yet.

No matter what you have written in the last subsection, or what you have written as you traveled on our joyful journey through this book and workbook, always remember what Walt Disney said, "Keep moving forward toward your dreams." Never give up! Don't quit! *Until you are "the late" you, it is never too late for you to achieve success!*

6) Lifetime Role Models: Be Mike or be *like* Mike. Again, using Michael Jordan as an example, in a famous Nike commercial, everyone was told, "Be like Mike." After he retired, NBA fans were all wondering, "Who will be the next Michael Jordan?"

Here is my advice. When idolizing lifetime role models, always remember, do not set out to be the next Mr. or Ms. X. Instead, *make it your life's goal to be the first/best you! It is the only part you will ever be able to play perfectly!*

Remember, you are A Perfect You! You were literally born to play the part of your life! So play it! If you do not play and live it, then all human history will miss out on you!

I learned this life lesson as follows: From 1981-1987, I was a camper at Interlochen National Arts Camp. I was a drama major. One summer, I was in a production of Hamlet. Was I Hamlet? No. A thousand times, no! But I was Francisco: a guard. I will never forget the director; he was wonderful. He made everyone feel important. Early on in the rehearsal process he called me over for one of his little chats. He said, "Okay. You are a guard. In the grand scheme of things, this may not seem like a big deal. But, even though you are not a lead part, *you are the leadoff man!* You have the first line of the play! And if you do not open up your mouth, and say your line with all the clear diction, commitment, and enthusiastic energy it deserves, then the greatest piece of playwriting known to human history does not start! I need to know what you will do!" I said, "Wow! I'll do it GREAT!"

For me this direction was huge! My feelings of self-worth, which only a moment ago, were marginal at best, now ballooned beyond belief! So I memorized my minor lines as if I was major! And when it came time to stand and unfold myself, I said every line, hit every mark, and I was the best Francisco: A Guard I could be. Whenever you play your real-life parts, no matter how minor they may be, or not be, and you do it with commitment and a positive, alive attitude, you gloriously grow into the major leader of your life. Diligently doing this is truly a holistic, honorable, and abundantly humanitarian act of self-centered altruism! *Promise yourself, "In the play of my life, I will always be the lead-er!"*

7) Love and Lotto. This is an anecdotal story, which perfectly illustrates my advice. There was an old man, who all his life had been obsessively fixated on winning the lottery. Every birthday wish he made and every, "If a genie were to give you three wishes ..." question, his answer always focused on winning the Mega-Millions Power-Ball, big money game, and "living happily ever after."

Well one day, when he is very old and very gray, he hears a whispering voice, which sounds similar to the voice Kevin Costner hears in *The Field of Dreams*. The old man thinks the voice says, "If you pray, you will win." So, of course he gets extremely excited. He immediately falls to his knees and starts to pray with all the energy and enthusiasm he can muster. Unfortunately, he is so obsessed with his delusional daydream, he stops doing everything else except praying. And after a few, non-stop days, he dies! Then, when he arrives in his version and vision of an afterlife, he hears the voice once again! Only this time, he hears it loud and clear. It says, "Oh! Old man! I said if you *play* you will win!"

Clearly the old man's post-mortem amplification and his subsequent, unfortunate clarification, comes far too late. But, I hope for you, the point here is not falling on deaf, or already dead, ears. I hope you ultimately understand, you can not simply sit on the sidelines, do nothing, and expect to be successful. You have to take action if you want to reveal your divine dreams and reach your golden goals. *And especially in the games of love and life, you have to play if you want to win!* And as far as you, "living happily ever after," I believe that state of doing is a lot less dependent on the amount of money you have in your wallet, as it is decidedly determined, by the amount of light and love you have in your heart.

Get GIGSS

In the curtain call of this book, you have read through Character Conclusions and Character Continuations. And now you have fourteen more concepts to think about and apply in your daily life. However, my advice is to go far beyond thinking. Start dramatically discussing. In short, get GIGSS (Gather In Group Support Systems).

Collect all your collaborators into enlightened ensembles. If you are a teenager, create *The Breakfast Club* commitment to character cliques. If you are an adult, create group support circles. Either way, find like-minded individuals and gather them together. Form informal federations and coalitions. Doing this on a consistent basis not only adds strength to your character's cause, but it is also an always at the ready resource for all its participants. And because these great groups commonly provide priceless professional networking and particularly positive personal accountability and outstanding opportunities.

I also highly recommend you see the movie *The Breakfast Club*. And for all teenagers a Breakfast Club-esque idea, is to propose to the principal of your school, he or she designate and do a Character Clique Switch Week. If you are given permission to perform such an event, do the following exercise:

Publishers Note: This exercise should only be done when facilitated by staff within the school and when everyone is aware of the exercise. The intent of the Cliques listed below is to open awareness about groups that may already exist or less-than-positive terms that can be assigned to a group of teenagers based on externally perceived characteristics. The focus of the work is not to reinforce these stereotypes but to increase awareness of the internal individuality of each and every person.

Exercise 17 - Character Clique Switch Week (Think of this exercise as a bigger picture parallel to my Elite Example Story at the end of Chapter 1: Character Crystallization!)

Step 1: Create a Cliques and Stereotypes List.

Here are several examples of common group labels outside observers see in schools.

Example Cliques and Stereotypes List

1. Sports Jocks, Jockettes, and Pep Rally Pros
2. Big Brainiacs
3. Un and Cool Crowders
4. Singers, Musicians, and Orchestra and Band Geeks
5. Artists, Actors, and Theater Casts and Crew
6. Rebels Without a Cause
7. Under and Overachievers
8. Smokers and Stoners
9. Loners and Last Picked
10. Bullies and Heart Breakers
11. Debate Team Talkers
12. Cheerleaders and Dance Team Talents
13. Prom King and Queen
14. Video, Card, Dice, and Role Player Gamers
15. Wall-Flower-Wannabes
16. Shop Specialists and Motor Metalheads
17. Student Council Club
18. Invisible Introverts and Extreme Extroverts
19. Anime, Comic Con, Goth, Punk, and Fantasy Friends
20. Math, Science, and Chess Clubbers
21. Meanies and Misunderstoods
22. Book Worms and Library Loungers
23. Phone Followers and Addicts
24. Social Media 24/7 Phone Posters, Texters, Likers, and Speed Scrollers

Step 2: Just as in Chapter 1: Character Crystallization!, make a list of twenty or more Outside Items and twenty or more Inside Items which describe you.

Step 3: Explain how and why each of these items gives you reason to associate yourself with any of the particular cliques on your list. Do you associate with more than one?

Step 4: On a separate piece of paper, write the names of your peers who are not in any of your friend groups. Use this list to pick your MAGIC matches—classmates you are curious and want to know more about.

Step 5: Have everyone turn in their response papers to the central office. Make sure each person's name and contact information is clearly printed at the top of each page. If the principal deems it necessary, have the school's guidance counselors and/or social workers go over everyone's responses to double check everything is set up for success and participants are taking things seriously, it is all being done safely, and they are all stretching themselves in the right ways.

Step 6: This step is done by the coordinators of the project. Along with the help of the school's guidance counselors and/or social workers, determine the designated peer matches for the exercise. Use the person's peer example list of someone they do not know much about to pinpoint the MAGIC matches.

Step 7: Provide each student with their MAGIC match notices. Share the twenty or so Outside Items and Inside Items lists from their match and include a Directions for the Week sheet. For the project to work, all the participants must receive these two items before the beginning of the week. Saturday at the latest.

Directions for the Week:

1. On Mind-Your-Match-Monday, anonymously observe your match.

2. On Tell-It-All-Tuesday, do introductions and spend some quality, get-to-real-ly-know-each-other time.

3. On Welcome-To-My-World-Wednesday, show each other your world. Talk and walk each other through a day in your life.

4. On Thankful-Thursday, find some small way to say, "Thank You!"

5. On Freaky Friday, come to school in costume, totally prepared for Character Clique Switch Day. You should look the look, talk the talk, and walk the walk. Spend the whole day as a member of your opposite clique.

6. Everyone wear a small sign, which presents the following information:

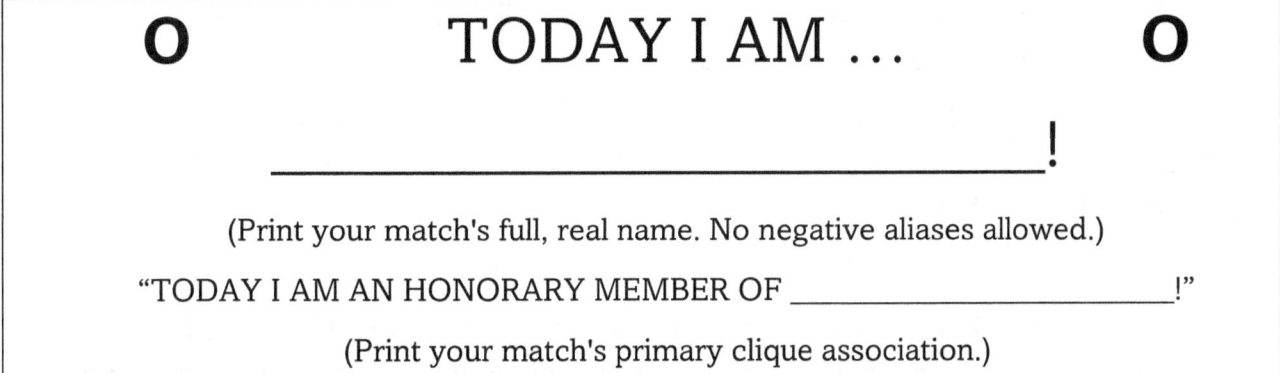

O   TODAY I AM ...   O

_____!

(Print your match's full, real name. No negative aliases allowed.)

"TODAY I AM AN HONORARY MEMBER OF _____!"

(Print your match's primary clique association.)

(Cut on the lines, laminate, punch out O holes, and wear around your neck.)

(Feel free to make a separate card for each different clique association.)

Step 7: After the Clique Switch Day is done, do two all-school, general assembly, debriefing days. One with all the students, and one with all the parents and/or guardians. [If deemed necessary, do two more debriefing meetings at least six months apart with both students and adults together.] At each event, the coordinators can facilitate open forum discussions, so everyone benefits from all the life lessons learned during the whole Clique Switch Week.

Step 8: Give students the option to write response reports and/or do Project Clique Switch presentations which describe what they learned from the whole experience. If possible, your school should save everything and bring it out from storage for class reunions. After an amount of time, you should see just how much has significantly changed and how much has steadfastly stayed the same. With the completion of this project, you and your classmates will have almost traveled full circle from what you accomplished back in Chapter 1. And in this chapter, you only have two more subsections to do.

Celebrate Family and Friends!

In the Nature vs. Nurture section in Chapter 1, you acknowledged the extensive contribution your family and friends have made in your life. In this subsection, you will choose and/or create several methods of showing your attitude of gratitude, and you will consciously celebrate your family and friends.

One seemingly obvious, yet commonly overlooked, method of showing gratitude, is mailing, "Thank You!" cards. Yes. It's true. Of course you can say thank you in person, or over the wireless-waves. But when you actually put something in writing, take the time to snail mail it, and the person real-ly receives a parcel piece of handwritten mail, in their mailbox, addressed to them, then no doubt it's extremely extraordinary. This is especially true in our modern age of highly specialized technology. With e-mailing, text messaging, smart phones, tablets/tech-notepads, and an abundance of Social Media Apps, etc., I personally think it is an absolute miracle any of us can even still remember how to write by hand at all.

Another method, which requires a little extra effort and personal creativity, is doing non-random acts of gratitude. Six examples of these, for-no-reason, not-a-special-day, activities and actions, are as follows:

Six Acts of Gratitude:

1) Do an extra chore, or a not-normally-your-job task, *without being asked and without drawing attention to the fact you did it!* This is a wonderful way to show great gratitude. It lightens the load for a mega-multitasking parent or guardian, and it shows you are real-ly paying attention to the world around you. And trust me, when someone, especially a teenager, displays any kind of non- egocentric, positively productive, altogether altruistic, tendency and/or behavior, this definitely does get nicely noticed. Even a small amount of effort will go a very long way and is usually very much appreciated.

2) Spend routine quality time together. They say, "Families who eat and play together, stay together." Even if you are only watching TV and talking about a local news program or seeing an early evening movie, the point is you are all doing it together and communicating with each other. This also works for weekly game nights, doing hobbies-at-home-time, reading and recreation, and planning and producing any and all activities.

    This rule also applies to love-a-lot friends. Eat school lunches together. Do club-time and group-dinners. And if you have long distance friends, make sure you talk on the phone and see each other online as much as possible.

3) Set spontaneous surprises for someone special. When you find yourself thinking of someone special, do something about it. Two ideas are make-a- morning and arrange an entertaining evening. On a day which is not the person's birthday or any other special occasion, arrive at school early and decorate their locker. Hang a BFF banner. Or on a non-anniversary day, plan a romantic rendezvous or create some clear calendar-time. This will give the recipient the opportunity to take some much-needed solo time.

4) Be trustworthy, true, accountable, and honorable. This may sound like a big picture idea, but you can easily show it with small picture actions. For example, build a reputation of being reliable and punctual. This way people learn, and subsequently come to *know* and expect, you are honorable to your word(s). This means you *always*

show up where and when you say you will. And you *always* show respect for the people who count on you to be where you say you will be, by being there on time.

5) Be a fantastic friend. Friends establish expectations and codes of conduct. There is no greater gift, then exceeding expectations and honoring codes.

6) Be familiar with your family. When you give a gift, or decide to do something special for someone, make sure your gift or action is custom catered and specifically selected for that particular person. One of the best examples of this idea, is inspired by the origin story of this book's title, and subsequently my whole business model! It is as follows: One post-college summer, I was a country club golf caddie. Now, I am not a great golfer. But I am a great caddie. So on the course I carried the bags, walked the walk, talked the talk, and thanks to my parents, looked the part. For when I got the job, they gave me a great gift that, well, fit me perfectly! It was a *TaylorMade*™ golf brand name, logo hat! Because after all, *I am Taylor Made!* With this hat on my head, my mind made a little logical leap up, and thought up, *TaylorED Time!*

My bottom-line paradigm for this subsection is as follows: I believe your life will be a thousand times easier, holistically more happy, and sensationally more successful, if you are able to do these non-random acts of gratitude. And that my friends is, as the Disney song from *Hercules* says, "The Gospel Truth."

Create Unity and Community!

When you organize your family and friends into life affirming GIGSS you are positively planning and productively planting seeds of unity and community. To tender these seeds, you need to develop all the character traits, which are required to be a conscientious gardener. You need to put in the time, and do the work, so the sown seeds can thrive and grow. The following two *Andrewism* poetry pieces illustrate my global perspective.

The Planetarians!

We Are All Infinite At Birth. We Are All A Plethora Of Possibilities!
We Are All Individual Worlds. We Are All-Encompassing Complete Creations!
We Are All Indigenous Peoples. We Are All A Community Of Cultures!
We Are All In Heart And Home. We Are All Holistically Complete Organisms!
We Are All Destined To Be Defined. We Are All Determined By Our Differences!
We Are All Evolutionarily Equal. We Are All SOUL-Full Samers!
We Are All Honorable To Our Heritage. We Are All Universal In Our Unity!
We Are All Earthlings. We Are All Planetarians!

A One-Sided World!

Stupid-Isms:
There Are Six People Populated Continents
    [North America - South America - Europe - Asia - Africa - Australia]
All With Fundamental Anti-Nationalisms!
There Are Five Major Organized Belief Systems
    [Christianity - Hinduism - Islam - Judaism - Buddhism]
All With Anti-Other-Religionisms!
There Are Four Special Needs Categories
    [Physical - Mental - Emotional - Learning]
All With Anti-Disabilityisms!
There Are Three Ways Of Desire
    [Hetero - Homo - Bi]
All With Anti-Orientationisms!
There Are Two Sexes
    [Male - Female]
Both With Susceptibility To Sexisms!
There Is One Race
    [Human]
Which Stupidly Subjects Itself To Racism!
    Now Listen To This Total Truth!
    We All Live On One Spherical Globe!
    I Beg You Remember Your Math!
    A.K.A. The Other Universal Language!
    I Am Talking Other Than The Arts!
    In Geometry Terms, The Undeniable Definition,
    For This Particular Planetary Point, ... Is,
    Your Home Is A One-Sided World!
    After a quick post view, you can go to Chapter 7: Behind the Scenes and Epilogue!

Post View

Well it's a-bow-t time! Yes! Finally we have come to the end of *our* journey! And it's about time you got here! And absolutely it is about time for you to take a big-time bow. Or at the very least, give yourself a pleasant pat on the back. Because let's face facts here. You have come a very long way!

So for a moment, look back with self-admiration!

You have completed the following two sections:

- Character Conclusions
- Character Continuations

And you have completed the following three subsections:

- Get GIGSS
- Celebrate Family and Friends!
- Create Unity and Community!

And you have completed the following exercise:

- Character Clique Switch Week

And you have completed two more of The 16 Secrets Of Success.

14. Get GIGSS (Gather In Group Support Systems). Take total responsibility for your life. Make a commitment to playing the lead-er part of *Your Life!* Live your life so self-improvement and acts of altruism are synonymous!

I remind you of the following four perfect points: One, you have taken total responsibility for your life and you have acknowledged your own response-abilities! Two, you have signed a Character Commitment Contract! Three, you have promised yourself, *"In the play of my life, I will always be the Lead-er!"* And four, you have written your versions of My Mission Statement and My Purpose In Life Paragraph, My Definition Of Success Story, and My Funeral, Epitaph, and Eulogy.

And with all these *written* documents, you have your future ambitions clearly mapped out in front of you. And when your mind's eye engages in creative visualization, you will already have created a visionary, picturesque path for you to travel. You will be completely confident, everything will lead you, to your best self's, perfect, Promised Land Life!

15. Celebrate family and friends! Create unity and community! Tap into your SOUL (Spirit Of Ultimate LOVE (Living Only Vibrant Energies))! Live the Life FANTASTIC (Full And Novel, Thriving And Successful, Totally In Control)!

You have followed through on your attitude of gratitude and you know six, un-random acts of gratitude you can easily produce on your own. And now you know how you need to be a conscientious gardener when it comes to your sowed seeds of unity and community. And finally, you have read two of my *Andrewisms*, poetry pieces, entitled *The Planetarians!* and *A One Sided World!* And now, you are more than ready, to live the life FANTASTIC!

AND ... You have done all these things successfully! YOU GO! YOU ARE THE CHARACTER!

Okay. Now turn the page. There you will find this book's last lines, in the short, sweet, and celebratory sentiments of Chapter 7: Behind the Scenes and Epilogue!

CHAPTER 7:
BEHIND THE SCENES AND EPILOGUE!

This is the final fanfare! It is time to tap into your SOUL and live the life FANTASTIC!

All right! Action! Scene …

The presentized news of the day is *our* journey has come to an end. It is time for *your* journey to begin. In short, "IT IS PARTY TIME!" You have organized, and faithfully found your GIGSS. You have celebrated family and friends! And you have played your part in the global/world scheme, of helping create unity and community! So now throw yourself a massive, enlightened ensemble, life cast party! If you can get in touch with any, or all, of your dinner guests and LRMs, then by all means, invite them all to the party!

At the party, have a Wall of Fame. Hang all your exercise results, and any other paperwork you have generated, while following this process, and walking the path of this particular self-help book and workbook. Post everything. At one end, start with your Fact Foundation PIES Chart and Your Holistic Resumé. At the other end, finish with your My Character Commitment Contract, My Mission Statement and My Purpose In Life Paragraph, My Definition Of Success Story, and My Funeral, Epitaph, and Eulogy.

And next, with as much pomp and circumstance as is humanly possible, create a ceremonial presentation. Make a promise of personal production. And make this promise to everyone who will willingly witness! *This is your empowering epilogue!*

SHOUT IT OUT LOUD AND CLEAR SO EVERYONE CAN HEAR!

I DO SOLEMNLY SWEAR AND PROMISE:
I WILL BE THE CAPTAIN OF MY CHARACTER'S CREATION!
I WILL PLAY THE LEAD-ER ROLE OF MY LIFE!
I WILL TAP INTO MY SOUL (SPIRIT OF ULTIMATE LOVE)!
I WILL LOVE (LIVE ONLY VIBRANT ENERGIES)!
I WILL LIVE THE LIFE FANTASTIC
(FULL AND NOVEL, THRIVING AND SUCCESSFUL, TOTALLY IN CONTROL)!

And finally do the last of The 16 Secrets of Success.

16) Presentize yourself! Go back to number one. Start over!

Now presentize yourself … again! See yourself at the summit of your New and Improved, self-helped self! Then, dramatically do what Jim Henson, the innovative and inspirational courageous creator of The Muppets, so eloquently empowered us all to do. He said, "Take what you've got and fly with it!"

GOOD LUCK IN ALL OF YOUR LIFE'S CHARACTER CREATIONS!
THANK YOU FOR READING AND DOING EVERYTHING!
YOUR CHARACTER CREATION COACH
AND ENTERTAINING EDUCATOR,

Andrew S. Taylor

A+ 🙂

AN ADDITIONAL A+  EXTRA EPILOGUE!

TaylorED Time: Self-Help Book & Companion Workbook
TODAY IS OUR BIRTHDAY! 4/2/2024 WE ARE 21 YEARS OLD!

Apparently our single parent, Andrew S. Taylor, started writing us on 4/2/2003! And to this we say, "WOW! It's amazing how far we've come!?" [And it's precisely this traversing of time I want to talk about now.] The publishing of these two books, along with my ten children's books, has been a life-long dream come true. And the reality of this journey has been a grandiose growth experience of extremely epic empowerment. Time and time again, there were physical, intellectual, emotional, and spiritual downs, ups, and life-speed learning curves that when all put together made all my miraculous manifestations appear as a six-star roller coaster ride of collaboratively crazy creativity. Time and time again I was told to lean into the experience of when life happens in place of plans and how I should continue my calm, feel my heart-full faith, and tenaciously trust the whole publishing process. And now, all my wonderful words cannot completely and competently express my attitude of gratitude toward my GracePoint Publisher family, my illustrator, my website designer, and all my lifetime of family and friends who have holistically helped me masterfully make my life, the universe, and everything so positively productive. And with all twelve books in hand, I find myself fully forging feelings for my future. I see it all as a positive paradigm of potential and I am absolutely alive with anticipation of abundance!

THANK YOU!!

ALIVINGLY42!!

ANDREW S. TAYLOR

A+ ☺

ABOUT THE AUTHOR

Andrew S. Taylor holds two BSED degrees in Pre-K-12, Elementary and Secondary Education Theater/Speech. As a self-employed entrepreneur, he is a teenage through adult Life Enrichment Teacher, Creativity Workshop Facilitator, Special Event Public Speaker, and Personal/Professional Life Coach/Consultant. He is equally proficient with individuals, couples, and large-scale groups. At Interlochen National Arts Camp, he was Divisional Honor Camper ('87 H.S.B. Theater Major) and Honor Cabin Counselor ('05 & '07). He was his university's Muppet Mascot, The OU Bobcat, a Pre-K-12 Child Care Teacher/Program Director for eight years, and also The Children's Department Supervisor & Storytime Reader, at a super-sized Barnes & Noble, for four years.

When not every day, enthusiastically engaged in creative writing, his hobbies include collating his colossal collection of Movies & TV Shows (2,800+DISKS!), making beaded jewelry (pins, necklaces, and friendship bracelets), and acting in Community Theater. Mr. Taylor lives in Ann Arbor, MI, and can be contacted at

OTHER BOOKS BY ANDREW S. TAYLOR

TaylorED Time Workbook: How to Be the Captain of Your Character's Creation

This is a companion workbook specifically designed with a duel productive purpose. Within its poignant pages, you will find several supportive tools to help you systematically succeed at achieving all your golden goals, constructing your creative character, and when used in tandem with the TaylorED Time self-help system, ALIVING-LY Living [Your Best] Life FANTASTIC!

The first productive purpose is to give all the extra space you need to complete and/or redo the book's exercises. The second is to show how to begin and keep a character creation journal. This is a terrific tool for facilitating personal, great-gratitude-nal growth, and ensuring supreme self-improvement. And for the creation of this item, all ingredients are included. You will draw inspiration from special, section-specific quotes, original *Andrewism* poetry pieces, and positively picturesque, professional photography by Carole A. Fletcher. Then you will describe, in safe-spaces for healthy handwritings, your true-mind/heart's thoughts and feelings.

This way, with this workbook, you will wonderfully do the work! You will expertly and efficiently profile your personal progress as you tenaciously travel though the joy-full journey that is YOUR TaylorED Time LIFE! A+:)

Children's Books

BIRDS!

Within these poignant pages, you will read about and review the colorful and complete world of all our feathered friends. See birds from far and near and explore their extensive, worldwide diversities. In the end, you will recognize and learn, despite all their differences, they are all still first and foremost, foundationally, one family of

birds! Yes it is true: each individual is special and unique. And so, also thus, in perfect parallel, they are all just like us!

Author Andrew S. Taylor and Illustrator James G. Martin take you on this vibrant and visual display of diversity of all the spectacular spectrum of beautiful birds. And you will ultimately see, how all that in totality, transparently translates into reality, to the whole planetary population of humanity, all around our wonderful world!

The Phenomenal Phoenix!

Within these poignant pages, you will effortlessly explore the expanded dictionary definition and the everlasting legend of The Phenomenal Phoenix! This beautiful bird will teach you much more than merely magical flying. Its spectacular story will show you how to take what you've got and fly with it!

Author Andrew S. Taylor and Illustrator James G. Martin bring this magical bird, and life lesson, ALIVE! Delve deeper between the lines. Go beyond the fictional fiery feathers. Discover how inside all of us there is a soaring spirit of strength that fortifies our very real and always at the ready, regal resilience. And with those character qualities, any and all adversity can be overtly overcome!

Something Small

Within these poignant pages, you will see how the something small, simple little things, do make a miraculous, dramatic difference.

Author Andrew S. Taylor and Illustrator James G. Martin subtlety show how the small, individual items, fantastically fit, into the big, beautiful, perfect picture. And so positively prove, everything and everyone, in our most wonderful world, most definitely and decidedly, matters!

A Cloud & The Eye of the Beholder

Within these poignant pages, we will explore how one sees... a cloud. Do you adult-ly and definitively define a cloud scientifically, as an accumulation of water vapor? Or do you child-ly and simply see a bunny's cottontail or a dramatic dragon's spiny sail? And maybe, most importantly, can you see both these things, both at the same time? YES! YES YOU CAN!

Author Andrew S. Taylor and illustrator James G. Martin delicately depict how we gradually grow up, seeing the world based on our beholder's eyes. They simply show how one should always sing and dance in all the puddles one can find. And how, with both eyes open, one should always anticipate all the rainbows and sunrays, which will soon break through the clouds, and illuminate your life!

Mommy, Am I BEAUTIFUL?

Within these poignant pages, a lovely little girl learns the life lesson of what is really the difference between being *externally*, purposely pretty, and *internally* doing the long list of high-quality character traits that make up the word BEAUTIFUL. As her older sister is getting ready for Prom, she is sent to learn this life lesson from Mom, the same way it has been passed down through generations.

Author Andrew S. Taylor and Illustrator James G. Martin address the intrinsic and introspective idea, in storybook form, that beauty comes from the inside. Whether it be her first day of school or for a special occasion, like a picturesque Prom, what matters most is what she is internally made of, and what are the core content qualities, of her truly confident character.

LULLABY-ed Child

Within these poignant pages, are fantastic frames artistically availed and rightly ready for fabulous photos. And also, the tender text is a simply sweet, lovely LULLABY sublimely set to melodic music. Use the professionally provided sheet music for yourself or hear the author sing it using a digital download. And for sure, your child will surrender to serene sleep.

Author Andrew S. Taylor and Illustrator James G. Martin colorfully create a new type of children's book. They provide a soft song to sing and cutely color-full frames, for you, the reader, to fill with your child's family photos. So, if (or when) digital technology, computers, the cloud, or our phones fail, your life's magical memories can be tangibly taken and productively put into a very real, picturesque place.

Sitting in the Lap of Love!

Within these poignant pages, is a short and sweet story of a magical memory: Mom making the safest of all spaces, a loving lap. Every year Mother's Day is in mid-May. With this book you can say, "It is every day!" The author shouts out a big, "THANK YOU!" to his mom. And you too, can simply show and greatly give gratitude to your mom. Or you can say these same sentiments to your daughter, daughter-in-law, any already mom, or any very-soon mom-to-be.

Author Andrew S. Taylor and Illustrator James G. Martin write right words and put into perfect pictures a love-full wonderful walk down a little lad's and a magnificent Mom's memory lane. They set the scene and all is seen. And yes, this book may be dedicated to Andrew's mom, but it is also a necessary nod to all nice neighbors, grandmothers, Mr. Moms, and noteworthy nurturers who help children feel soulfully safe and beautifully beheld.

Every Day is Mother's Day: Sitting in the Sunroom of My Sweetest Sanctuary

Within these poignant pages, is the subsequent sequel to *Sitting in the Lap of Love!* It is also a perfect prompt to start the art of scrapbooking. Just as *LULLABY-ed Child* provides places to put pictures, this book showcases small spaces for short sentimental stories. Mother and child can beautifully begin here, and lovingly learn, how to continue co-creating, happily-for-fun-ly, and forever-ever-after.

Author Andrew S. Taylor and Illustrator James G. Martin positively present a pair of books as beautiful bookends. The first book was set in the past. This second book is set in the present. Which makes it the greatest of gifts, for one to gratefully give, to your favorite, fantastic, miraculous mother. And as the art of scrapbooking can be a crafty activity that lasts for lifetimes, once started, mothers and children can share memories for millenniums.

A Perfect Day!

Within these poignant pages, is the origin story of one of my long-lifetime's most outstanding occupations: FISHING! Showing how it's always beyond its best when done with my Dad! I was eight years old, when I caught my first fish. Dad set up, showed, and explained everything. With my success, I was hooked! When I turned a teen, we went to Montana. It was my first "Only-US fishing trip." This is that sweet story.

Author Andrew S. Taylor and Illustrator James G. Martin tenderly tell and soulfully show a time-honored tradition: Father and son going fishing. And just like the movie *Field of Dreams* inspired countless calls of, "Hello Dad. Do you wanna have a catch?," they hope this book will cast out all its lines and catch hold of all angler hearts all around the world. They hope it inspires grandparents, parents, sons, and daughters to all find time to go fishing together, make magical memories, and ALIVINGLY live as many picturesquely Perfect Days as is pleasantly and positively possible!

Another Perfect Day! Every Day is Dad's Day

Within these poignant pages, is decades down the rivers' bends, making more memories and never knowing how (or when) the story ends. And after almost forty years it is this final fact that makes each newly made, magical memory so much more meaningful: For me, fishing is a soul-full-filling summer season. And family, friends, Mom, and Dad, are an all-day-every-day attitude of gratitude! THANK YOU FOR MY LIFE & MY LOVE!

Author Andrew S. Taylor and Illustrator James G. Martin now conclude their collection of ten children's books. [More might be made as ideas arise: coloring books, activity books, and children's coaching books.] But it's this final fishing book that's their last cast of this life's season of super sensational, successful stories. What comes next? Let's see what we can catch, using the inter-net! To You: Good Luck! & FANTASTIC Fishing!

www.ingramcontent.com/pod-product-compliance
Lightning Source LLC
Chambersburg PA
CBHW081002120626
46546CB00010B/2997